VEGAN YUM

THE SECRETS TO MASTERING PLANT-BASED COOKING

MEGAN SADD

Author of *30-Minute Vegan Dinners*
and creator of Carrots & Flowers

PAGE STREET
PUBLISHING CO.

PAGE STREET
PUBLISHING CO.

First published in 2020 by
Page Street Publishing Co.
27 Congress Street, Suite 105
Salem, MA 01970
www.pagestreetpublishing.com

Distributed by Macmillan, sales in Canada by The Canadian Manda Group.

24 23 22 21 20   1 2 3 4 5

ISBN-13: 978-1-64567-126-8
ISBN-10: 1-64567-126-7

Library of Congress Control Number: 2019957317

Cover and book design by Kylie Alexander for Page Street Publishing Co.
Photography by Megan Sadd
Illustrations by Linda Knight

Printed and bound in China

TO EVERYONE TAKING STEPS TOWARD A PLANT-BASED DIET.
EVERY MEAL IS A WIN, AND YOUR CHOICES MATTER.
I HOPE THIS BOOK HELPS YOU FALL IN LOVE WITH
VEGAN COOKING AS MUCH AS I HAVE!

BUFFALO TEMPEH BLTS (PAGE 136)

TABLE OF CONTENTS

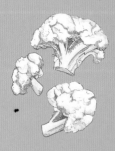

SAVORY
A CRASH COURSE IN PLANT-BASED UMAMI FLAVORS

FRESH
HOW TO BALANCE BRIGHT AND DELICATE FLAVORS

SPICY
THE JOY OF HEAT

SWEET
THE ART OF VEGAN BAKING AND ICE CREAM MAKING

BREAKFAST BURRITOS WITH EGGY
TOFU SCRAMBLE (PAGE 70)

FOREWORD

The very first time Megan cooked for me, I took one bite and told my husband it was over. I was moving in with Megan. The dish she made was an incredibly savory, nutty, eclectic mix of serious vegan yum. It was the BBQ Tempeh Soul Bowl from her first cookbook, *30-Minute Vegan Dinners*. It had me hooked on Megan's jaw-dropping creativity and talent from the moment the flavors danced across my tongue. The meal she made also reminded me of the types of flavors and protein-packed goodness I had started my plant-based journey on, a few years out from the 2012 London Olympic Games. As one of the world's best cyclists vying for a spot on the Olympic team, most people discouraged any change to my then animal-based diet just years out from the Games, but I was committed. I created easy, nutrient-dense and flavorful plant-based meals that both fueled and amplified my performance. While none were as tantalizing as Megan's food, the concept was the same: simple, tasty and healthy. *Vegan YUM* will help you create satisfying, delicious, simple, energy-promoting food for you and your family in the most delightful way.

Megan's food is simply stunning. Despite this, it's actually so easy to replicate, which for me is crucial. I can drool over cookbooks all day but if I can't make a meal in 20 minutes, I'll never do it. Each recipe is crafted with flavor and nutrition in mind. From her Miso Rainbow Veggie Bowl (page 105) and the Backyard BBQ Chicken Bowl (page 23) to the meaty Portobello-Walnut Bolognese (page 26) and the Spicy Garlic Ramen (page 132), the flavors never get old. There is truly a taste for everyone here. Megan's book is a wonderful resource for you to triumph in the kitchen. All of her recipes will put you in the hero seat, whether you're serving a family dinner or hosting a lavish party.

A quick note for the cheese-lovers out there: Megan makes crazy good cheese (that happens to be plant-based). Follow her recipes, and you will master the art of transforming just five ingredients into the gooiest, yummiest cheeses to accompany any dish or simply snack on. Her cheese recipes alone make this book an essential resource in any home kitchen.

Above all, what I love most about Megan's meals is the pure jubilation. When I hang out with her in the kitchen, there is always this abundant joyful energy. Her passion is making plant-based food and teaching the world not only how wonderful the end result can be, but how loving and beautiful the process is.

This book brings me joy, and I hope it brings you joy, too. More importantly, I hope you actually cook from it and use these recipes to nourish yourself and your family. We all have the potential for greatness, and while I'm not saying her meals will make you an Olympian (but who knows?), they can definitely give you more energy and simply make you feel fantastic in your body. Enjoy exploring these recipes, bookmarking your favorites and sharing with others. If you're anything like me, you'll flip first to that 5-minute cheese recipe (page 38)!

Dotsie Bausch

Olympic Silver Medalist 2012
Founder of Switch4Good.org
Star of the film *The Game Changers*

CRISPY TOFU FISH TACOS (PAGE 24)

INTRODUCTION

When I first discovered plant-based eating at fifteen, I was fascinated. Discovering that every flavor and texture I loved to eat could be replicated with plants—vibrant, colorful, life-giving PLANTS—it just made sense. I knew then and there that this was my path.

While I didn't adopt a fully plant-based diet right away, the spark and passion I had for cooking with plants led me to a two-decade-long exploration of vegan cuisine. I worked in vegan restaurants, pored over every plant-based cookbook I could find and spent years in the kitchen experimenting, long before I ever shared a recipe online or wrote my first cookbook, *30-Minute Vegan Dinners*.

The food that I make—and all the culinary knowledge and techniques I've painstakingly crafted over the years—has always come down to one thing: pleasure seeking. I love creating succulent textures that melt in your mouth and flavor profiles that dance across your tongue. It's a primal satisfaction. My food is generously seasoned, well-balanced, creative and fun. I'm best known for healthy comfort food and amazing vegan cheese recipes.

These days, I get to share my passion for plant-based cooking with millions—at conferences and summits, on national TV and in newspapers and magazines all over the world. I'm so, so grateful for that! With my second book, I'm delighted to share an offering I've been dreaming up for years, a truly comprehensive guide to vegan food, in addition to a drool-worthy cookbook!

In *Vegan YUM*, I've distilled everything I know into 75 genius recipes to help you master plant-based cooking. Each recipe is driven by flavor, technique, thoughtful execution and a strong desire to make you go, "YUMMMM," when you taste it!

In **MEATY**, we'll dive into the ways you can create satisfying vegan meals with meaty flavors and textures, like flaky Classic British Fish 'n' Chips (page 20) and juicy Meatball Gyros (page 16)! In **CHEESY**, you'll learn the secrets to making incredible vegan cheese at home, including Cashew Caprese Mozzarella (page 58) and Smoky Gouda (page 42). **SAVORY** focuses on creating meals with deep umami flavors, often one of the biggest challenges to do well in vegan cuisine. Think Artichoke-Pesto Veggie Pizza (page 82) and Mushroom-Asparagus Breakfast Crepes (page 89).

FRESH is a celebration of bright flavors, like Pan-Seared Tempeh with Lemon-Parmesan Cream (page 94), while **SPICY** is all about the joy of heat, featuring a to-die-for Cajun Caesar with Blackened Chickpeas (page 120) and so much more! **SWEET** offers elevated classics like Avocado-Mint Chip Ice Cream (page 149) and boldly unexpected, impressive desserts, like Fudge Brownie Baked Alaska (page 154).

Each chapter is led with illustrated guides to help you discover the joy and ease of plant-based cooking and feel confident in your ability to create vegan masterpieces in the kitchen. The only limit is your imagination!

With love, *Megan Sadd*

MEATY

THE BEST PLANT-BASED MEAT SWAPS

MUSHROOMS

Meaty, juicy, savory and versatile. Use portobellos, criminis or shiitake in place of beef or pork (Portobello-Walnut Chorizo Hash [page 123] and Portobello-Walnut Bolognese [page 26]). Oyster mushrooms make a great swap for seafood (Spring Linguine with King Oyster Scallops [page 97] and One-Pot Vegan Jambalaya [page 127]).

CAULIFLOWER

This toothsome veggie works well in place of mild-flavored meats, like chicken and seafood. It can replace wings (page 124)! It can be ceviche (page 110)! What can't cauliflower do?

CHICKPEAS

Beyond making falafel and hummus, chickpeas are fantastic to throw in nearly any dish for heartiness. They can even be mashed and made into crispy vegan chicken patties (page 12)! Save the liquid from canned chickpeas—also called aquafaba—to use as a vegan egg replacer.

JACKFRUIT

A South Asian fruit perfect for making pulled vegan meats. Look for cans of jackfruit in water or brine—not juice, which is sweet. Jackfruit is typically sold in Asian markets and health food stores. Try it in Meat Lover's BBQ Pulled Jackfruit (page 15), Meal-Prep Jackfruit Carnitas (page 30) and Mole Jackfruit Tacos (page 34).

HOW TO MAKE HEARTY, SUCCULENT MEALS THAT WOW

I want to let you in on a secret. It's actually plants that make meat taste good in the first place! Imagine eating an unseasoned chicken breast. Rather bland, wouldn't you say? That's because it's the herbs, spices and seasonings that really make meat shine. Now that we have the flavor aspect covered, let's move on to texture. There's a wide array of plants that can deliver all the juicy, meaty, chewy textures you crave, minus the actual meat. Here are a few of my faves!

TOFU

Firm or extra-firm works best for meat alternatives. Press some of the water out of your tofu to achieve the best flavor and texture. Fall in love with tofu when you make Baked Tofu Club Sandwiches (page 74) and Marinated Tofu Poke Soba Bowls (page 106)!

LENTILS & WALNUTS

A match made in heaven! With a perfect blend of heartiness and crunch, lentils and walnuts can replace beef in sauces, chilis, tacos, lasagna and so much more! Find them together in the Epic Veggie Burgers (page 29) and One-Pot Lentil-Walnut Baked Ziti (page 53).

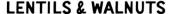

SOY CURLS

Soy curls are made from soybeans and provide a shockingly realistic meaty texture. I love using them to make vegan chicken. Find them online or in the earthiest of natural markets. Pick up a few bags to make Vietnamese Mango Chicken Bowls (page 98), Backyard BBQ Chicken Bowls (page 23) and Tacos de Pollo (page 19).

TEMPEH

Made from fermented soybeans, tempeh is nutty, crunchy, high in protein and super easy to prepare. Tempeh tastes best in dishes that have a slight sweetness to them, like bacon, BBQ and even salmon! Try it in Pan-Seared Tempeh with Lemon-Parmesan Cream (page 94) and spicy Buffalo Tempeh BLTs (page 136).

Note that dark spots on tempeh are a natural result of the fermentation process.

VEGAN GROUND BEEF

Once a specialty ingredient, vegan ground beef can now be found in most grocery stores. Use as a 1:1 replacement in any recipe calling for beef. Try it in Meatball Gyros (page 16), Spicy Breakfast Sausage Muffins (page 33) and Italian Meatloaf (page 37).

CRISPY SOUTHERN CHICKPEA SANDWICHES

Did you know that a humble can of chickpeas can be transformed into crispy chicken sandwiches? And they're gluten-free? It's a vegan miracle! The gluten-free MVP of this recipe is psyllium husk. This acts as a binder but keeps the patties lighter than traditional vegan meats, which often rely on vital wheat gluten for a meaty texture.

PREP TIME: 15 MINUTES • COOK TIME: 30 MINUTES • YIELD: 6 SANDWICHES

CHICKPEA PATTIES
2½ tbsp (12 g) psyllium husk

½ cup (120 ml) water

1 (14-oz [400-g]) can chickpeas

2 tbsp (30 ml) grapeseed or other mild oil

1 cup (50 g) panko or gluten-free panko breadcrumbs

1½ cubes (6 g) vegan chicken bouillon

1 tbsp (9 g) nutritional yeast

1 tbsp (15 ml) apple cider vinegar

1 tbsp (3 g) poultry seasoning

1½ tsp (3 g) smoked paprika

1 tsp garlic powder

¼ tsp black pepper

Cooking spray

BREADING
¼ cup (31 g) rice or all-purpose flour

¼ cup (13 g) panko or gluten-free panko breadcrumbs

2 tbsp (25 g) brown sugar

1 tbsp (8 g) Cajun seasoning

1 tsp onion powder

¼ tsp sea salt

Dash of cayenne

FOR SERVING
6 small vegan sandwich buns

6 tbsp (90 ml) vegan mayo

Lettuce, sliced tomato and sliced pickles

Preheat the oven to 375°F (191°C). Line a baking sheet with parchment paper. In a small bowl, combine the psyllium husk and water. Mix well and set aside to thicken.

Drain the chickpeas, reserving the liquid (aquafaba) in a shallow bowl. Rinse the chickpeas, then put them in a medium mixing bowl. Add the grapeseed oil and mash well with a potato masher until no whole chickpeas remain. Don't overmash. You want some texture left.

Add the panko breadcrumbs, bouillon, yeast, vinegar, poultry seasoning, paprika, garlic powder and pepper to the chickpeas. Mix well with your hands. Add the psyllium and water mixture and mix until evenly combined. Divide the chickpea mixture into six even balls. Flatten them into patties, about a ½ inch (12 mm) thick.

Make the breading. Combine the flour, breadcrumbs, brown sugar, Cajun seasoning, onion powder, salt and cayenne in a second shallow bowl. Mix well.

Dip each patty in the aquafaba, then coat them in the flour mixture. Place the breaded patties on the baking sheet. Spray with cooking oil.

Bake for 30 minutes, or until golden brown and crisp. Flip the patties halfway through the cook time. Spray both sides with more cooking oil when you flip them.

Toast the buns. Build your sandwiches with your desired toppings and a chickpea patty!

FRESH TIP!

Ground psyllium husk can be found in the supplement section of most health food stores, in the fiber aisle.

MEAT LOVER'S BBQ PULLED JACKFRUIT WITH AVOCADO SLAW

If you're looking for a vegan meat recipe that can fool even the biggest meat lovers in your life, this is the one! The secret to getting the meatiest texture and best flavor is to first cook the jackfruit on the stove with spices. Then a nice, long bake time makes the jackfruit chewy, meaty and absolutely perfect.

PREP TIME: 15 MINUTES • COOK TIME: 50 MINUTES • YIELD: 4 LARGE SANDWICHES

BBQ PULLED JACKFRUIT
3 (20-oz [567-g]) cans jackfruit (in water or brine, not juice)

1 tbsp (15 ml) grapeseed or other cooking oil

1 large yellow onion, finely chopped

4 cloves garlic, minced

3 tbsp (45 ml) apple cider vinegar

3 tbsp (45 ml) molasses

1 tbsp (15 ml) yellow mustard

2 tsp (2 g) dried thyme

2 tsp (10 ml) vegan Worcestershire sauce

1½ tsp (7 ml) liquid smoke

1 tsp chili powder

1 tsp smoked paprika

1 cup (240 ml) vegetable broth

½ cup (120 ml) tomato-based BBQ sauce, plus more for serving

AVOCADO SLAW
1 large avocado, mashed

2 tbsp (30 ml) white vinegar

1 tsp celery seed

2 tsp (10 g) organic sugar

Sea salt and black pepper, to taste

3 cups (210 g) shredded green cabbage

FOR SERVING
4 large vegan sandwich buns

2 tbsp (28 g) vegan butter (optional)

Preheat the oven to 400°F (204°C). Drain the jackfruit. Trim away the tough core pieces and remove the seeds. Roughly chop the jackfruit. This will help achieve the meaty, pulled texture.

In a large pan, heat the oil on medium-high. Sauté the onion for 1 to 2 minutes, or until it becomes slightly translucent. Add the garlic and cook for another minute or two. Stir in the jackfruit, then add the vinegar, molasses, mustard, thyme, Worcestershire sauce, liquid smoke, chili powder and paprika. Stir well.

Pour the vegetable broth into the pan, reduce the heat to medium and cover. Cook the jackfruit until all the liquid is absorbed, about 10 minutes. Stir occasionally.

Lightly oil a 9 x 13–inch (23 x 33–cm) glass or ceramic baking dish. Spread the jackfruit in the baking dish in an even layer. Place in the oven for 20 minutes, then take the pan out and pour the BBQ sauce over the jackfruit. Stir well until evenly combined, and use a fork to shred the jackfruit even more. Bake the jackfruit for another 20 minutes.

Meanwhile, make the avocado slaw. In a medium bowl, mash the avocado. Add the vinegar, celery seed, sugar, salt and pepper. Add the cabbage, and mix until evenly coated. Place in the fridge to chill.

Spread the buns with butter (if using), and toast them on a skillet or in a toaster oven. Assemble the sandwiches with a large scoop of jackfruit, avocado slaw and a drizzle of BBQ sauce on a bun. Serve with extra slaw.

FRESH TIPS!

Canned jackfruit can be found in many well-stocked grocery stores, health food stores and Indian and Asian markets. Baking the jackfruit in a glass or ceramic (not metal) pan will deliver a crispier texture.

The avocado slaw is best served fresh. If making the slaw ahead of time, it's best to swap the mashed avocado with ¼ cup (60 ml) of vegan mayo.

MEATBALL GYROS WITH CREAMY CASHEW TZATZIKI

These meatball gyros are juicy, full of flavor and made with pea-based vegan ground "beef." Vegan ground beef gives off more fat when cooking than regular beef, so developing a crust on the meatballs before finishing them in the oven helps to lock in the moisture and flavor. Save time by using Violife feta, or make your own with the recipe on page 62.

PREP TIME: 25 MINUTES • COOK TIME: 15 MINUTES • YIELD: 4 LARGE SERVINGS

MEATBALLS

Cooking spray

⅓ small yellow onion, very finely minced

3 cloves garlic, very finely minced

1 lb (454 g) vegan ground beef

¼ cup (23 g) mint leaves, finely chopped

4 oz (113 g) vegan feta, finely diced (store-bought or page 62)

2 tbsp (14 g) breadcrumbs or gluten-free breadcrumbs

2 tsp (4 g) ground cumin

1 tsp dried oregano

¼ tsp sea salt

¼ tsp red pepper flakes

CREAMY CASHEW TZATZIKI

1 cup (160 g) raw cashews, soaked for 6+ hours or boiled for 10 minutes

½ cup (120 ml) water

1 tbsp (15 ml) lemon juice, plus more to taste

¼ tsp salt, plus more to taste

1 large cucumber, grated

¼ cup (13 g) dill

¼ cup (15 g) parsley, plus more for garnish

¼ cup (23 g) mint leaves, finely chopped

FOR SERVING

4 pitas

1 cup (149 g) small tomatoes

Preheat the oven to 450°F (232°C). Spray a large pan with cooking oil and place it over medium heat. When the pan is hot, cook the onion and garlic for 1 to 2 minutes, until softened, then remove from the heat and set aside.

In large bowl, combine the vegan ground beef, mint, feta, breadcrumbs, cumin, oregano, salt and red pepper flakes. Mix until evenly combined. Use a melon scooper to portion 1-inch (2.5-cm) balls, then roll them tightly in your hands.

Place the pan back over medium heat. Spray with cooking oil, then add the meatballs. Cook until a thick crust forms on the meatballs, turning them frequently, about 5 to 6 minutes.

Meanwhile, make the tzatziki. Combine the cashews, water, lemon juice and salt in a high-speed blender. Blend until smooth and creamy, about 2 minutes. Taste the cream. Add more salt or lemon juice if the cream needs a bit more tang to achieve a yogurt-like flavor. Transfer the cream to a bowl. Stir in the cucumber, dill, parsley and mint. Cover and chill until ready to serve.

When the meatballs have a nice crust, transfer them to a baking sheet and bake for 6 minutes. Warm the pitas and halve the tomatoes. Wrap several meatballs, tomatoes and a large scoop of tzatziki in a warm pita.

WHOLE-FOOD PLANT-BASED OPTION—Line a baking sheet. Omit the vegan feta. Instead, mix 2 tablespoons (14 g) of ground flaxseed with 5 tablespoons (75 ml) of water. Replace the vegan ground beef with 1½ cups (297 g) of cooked or canned brown lentils and ⅓ cup (35 g) of walnuts. Pulse the lentils, walnuts, onion and garlic in a food processor until well combined but still a little chunky. In a bowl, combine the lentil mixture, flaxseed and water mixture and ¼ cup (27 g) of breadcrumbs with the mint and seasonings. Roll the dough into 1-inch (2.5-cm) balls. Put the balls directly on the lined baking sheet and into the oven. Don't brown on the stove first or they will fall apart. Bake for 15 to 17 minutes, turning the meatballs halfway through, until crisp on the outside and cooked through.

TACOS DE POLLO

How to make the easiest vegan chicken of all time: Hydrate soy curls in a mixture of near boiling water and tamari. The tamari gives the curls a strong but nondescript savory taste that you can build on to create different flavor profiles. Here, I've used a combination of cumin, chili powder, lime juice and green tomatillo salsa to create an authentic Mexican pollo flavor. Prepare to be amazed!

PREP TIME: 20 MINUTES • COOK TIME: 20 MINUTES • YIELD: 4 SERVINGS

8 oz (227 g) soy curls

3½ cups (840 ml) very hot water (see Fresh Tips!)

1½ cups (360 ml) tamari

1 white onion

5–6 cloves garlic

2 tsp + 2 tbsp (40 ml) grapeseed or avocado oil, divided

1 tbsp (6 g) cumin

1 tbsp (8 g) chili powder

4 tsp (20 ml) lime juice

½ cup (120 ml) green tomatillo salsa

FOR SERVING

10–12 corn tortillas

¼ cup (4 g) cilantro

1 lime

1 cup (70 g) shredded cabbage

½ cup (120 ml) green tomatillo salsa

1 cup (233 g) guacamole

1 cup (240 ml) vegan queso (optional, page 54)

MAKE IT LIGHTER—

Use 2 heads of butter lettuce or 1 small head of red cabbage in place of tortillas.

Put the soy curls, water and tamari in a bowl. Stir well and set aside to rehydrate for 10 minutes. Meanwhile, finely dice the onion. Set aside two-thirds of the onion to cook with the soy curls. Reserve the rest for garnish. Mince the garlic and set aside.

When the soy curls are hydrated, use a clean kitchen towel to wring them out. If they aren't squeezed properly, the excess liquid can result in a rubbery texture, so squeeze away! Chop the curls into bite-size pieces.

Put a pan over medium heat. Pour in 2 teaspoons (10 ml) of oil and tilt the pan to spread the oil. Add the onion and cook for about 2 minutes, until soft. Add the garlic. Stir and cook for another minute, then add the soy curls. Drizzle the remaining 2 tablespoons (30 ml) of oil over the soy curls and stir to coat.

Sprinkle the cumin and chili powder over the curls. Add the lime juice and stir. Cook for 8 to 10 minutes, until brown and crispy, stirring every 30 seconds or so. Add the salsa and mix well. This step adds flavor but will also make the soy curls a bit juicy. Cook for 3 to 4 minutes until the soy curls become slightly crispy again—stop to taste a piece. Scrape the bottom of the pan with a wooden spoon to prevent sticking.

Warm the tortillas. Chop the cilantro. Slice the lime into wedges. Build the tacos with a scoop of vegan pollo, onion, cilantro, cabbage, salsa, guacamole and a squeeze of lime juice. If you're feeling extra, try a little vegan queso on top!

FRESH TIPS!

Make sure the water to soak the soy curls in is very hot (close to boiling), or they'll take longer to hydrate.

Double the recipe to make easy tacos and burrito bowls throughout the week!

CLASSIC BRITISH FISH 'N' CHIPS

Eating a plant-based diet does NOT mean giving up your favorite meals—just swapping out some of the ingredients! Banana blossoms make the perfect stand-in for fish. Found in Asian markets or online, banana blossoms are the edible flowers that grow on banana trees. They have a flaky texture and mild flavor perfect for marinating with briny kelp, lemon and dill for an unbelievable seafood taste. Time in the freezer before frying ensures the blossoms will turn out extra crispy. Add a quick vegan tartar sauce for dipping, and you've got a bona fide fish-and-chips experience.

> PREP TIME: 15 MINUTES • COOK TIME: 20 MINUTES • YIELD: 2 TO 3 SERVINGS

FISH
1 (18-oz [510-g]) can banana blossoms

2 cups (480 ml) water

1 tbsp (12 g) kelp powder

1 tbsp (15 ml) lemon juice

1 tsp chopped dill

VEGAN TARTAR SAUCE
¼ cup (60 ml) vegan mayo

1 tbsp (10 g) cornichons, minced

2 tsp (20 g) capers, chopped

1 tsp white vinegar

½ tsp Dijon mustard

1 tsp fresh dill, chopped

Pinch of salt and pepper

BATTER
1 cup (240 ml) ice-cold beer (I use IPA)

1½ cups (188 g) all-purpose or rice flour, divided

1 tsp celery salt

1 tsp paprika

¾ tsp baking powder

¼ tsp pepper

Pinch of garlic powder

1 (16-oz [453-g]) bag frozen French fries

4 cups (960 ml) oil, for frying

Lemon wedges, for serving

Drain the blossoms, then wrap them in a clean kitchen towel. Squeeze out the brine. Combine the water, kelp powder, lemon juice and dill in a mixing bowl. Submerge the blossoms in the water. Cover and place in the freezer for 1 hour.

Meanwhile, make the vegan tartar sauce. Combine the mayo, cornichons, capers, vinegar, Dijon and dill. Season to taste with salt and pepper. Place in the fridge to chill. Wait 30 minutes, then preheat the oven to 400°F (204°C).

Put the beer and flour in the freezer for 10 minutes to chill. This will help keep the filets extra crispy when frying. Once it's chilled, mix 1 cup (125 g) of flour with the celery salt, paprika, baking powder, pepper and garlic powder. Mix well. Slowly add the beer to the flour mixture while stirring. Place the batter back in the freezer for 10 minutes so it stays ice-cold.

Bake the frozen fries for 20 minutes, or according to the package instructions. Add the remaining ½ cup (63 g) of flour to a plate. In a large, deep skillet, heat the oil to 365°F (185°C). Meanwhile, take the blossoms out of the freezer and drain.

Wrap the blossoms in another clean towel and squeeze out the marinade. Press the leaves together tightly to form a filet shape, then coat the blossoms with the remaining flour, making sure to get it into all the crevices. Working in batches, dunk each blossom in the batter, then fry until golden brown and crisp, about 4 minutes. Flip halfway through cooking. Drain on paper towels, then fry the second batch. Serve the filets with baked fries, tartar sauce and a squeeze of lemon.

FRESH TIPS!

Always fry in batches to avoid overcrowding the pan.

If the oil temperature drops, the filets can become greasy. I recommend heating the oil back up between batches. This will ensure the second batch is perfectly crisp. To test if the oil is hot enough, add a bit of salt. When it sizzles, it's ready!

BACKYARD BBQ CHICKEN BOWLS

These creamy, crunchy bowls are a celebration of the textures I love and the big, bold flavors I can't get enough of. We've got kale and quinoa for crunch, chopped pickles and onions for tang and the meatiest dang vegan BBQ chicken of all time. (Shout-out to soy curls!) Make a big batch for picnics, potlucks or to meal prep for the week. If you're making this for meal prep, slice the avocados fresh just before serving.

PREP TIME: 20 MINUTES • COOK TIME: 10 MINUTES • YIELD: 8 SERVINGS

8 oz (227 g) soy curls

4 cups (960 ml) very hot water

¾ cup (180 ml) tamari or low-sodium soy sauce

1 bunch curly kale

2 tbsp (30 ml) olive oil, divided

1 tbsp (15 ml) lemon juice

½ tsp salt

1 shallot, finely diced

4 cloves garlic, minced

2 tsp (4 g) smoked paprika

2 tsp (4 g) onion powder

2 tsp (10 ml) liquid smoke

1 tbsp (15 ml) apple cider vinegar

1 cup (240 ml) BBQ sauce

4 cups (740 g) cooked quinoa

2 (14-oz [400-g]) cans chickpeas, drained and rinsed

3 cups (447 g) cherry tomatoes, halved

1 cup (143 g) bread & butter pickles, chopped

½ red onion, finely diced

2 avocados, diced

FOR SERVING

¼ cup (4 g) cilantro or microgreens

1 cup (240 ml) BBQ sauce (optional)

1 cup (240 ml) vegan ranch or cashew cream (optional, page 93)

Put the soy curls, water and tamari in a bowl. Stir well and set aside for 10 minutes to rehydrate. Meanwhile, tear the kale from the stem and finely chop the leaves. In a large bowl, massage the kale with 2 teaspoons (10 ml) of olive oil, lemon juice and salt.

When the soy curls are plump, use a clean kitchen towel to wring them out. Excess liquid can give them a rubbery texture, so be sure to squeeze tight! Chop the curls into bite-size pieces or thin strips.

Put a pan over medium-high heat. When it's hot, coat the pan with 1 teaspoon of olive oil. Cook the shallot for about 1 minute, stirring once or twice. Add the garlic. Cook and stir for 30 seconds. Add the soy curls and the remaining 1 tablespoon (15 ml) of oil to the pan. Stir until they are well coated. Add the paprika, onion powder and liquid smoke. Stir well.

Cook the curls until golden brown and crisp, about 8 to 10 minutes, stirring every 30 seconds or so. Add the vinegar and BBQ sauce. Mix well, then cook for another minute, until the sauce gets very thick and sticky. Remove from the heat.

Add the quinoa, chickpeas, tomatoes, pickles and onion to the kale. Toss well. Divide among serving bowls. Top each bowl with a large scoop of BBQ soy curls and diced avocado. Finish with a few sprigs of cilantro or microgreens, extra BBQ sauce and a drizzle of ranch, if desired.

CRISPY TOFU FISH TACOS

When re-creating classic dishes with plants, it's important to remember that we are most drawn to qualities of the food rather than the foods themselves. As someone who's lived in LA for half of my life, I'm constantly craving fish tacos. But what I'm really craving is the tenderness of the fish and the crispy, savory exterior. Here, I used seaweed-marinated tofu for the fish and a well-seasoned flour blend for the coating, which makes a taco that definitely satisfies a fish taco craving!

See photo on page 8.

PREP TIME: 30 MINUTES • COOK TIME: 20 MINUTES • YIELD: 4 SERVINGS

TOFU FISH
12 oz (340 g) firm tofu
2 tbsp (30 ml) water
1½ tbsp (22 ml) soy sauce or tamari
1 tsp kelp powder
1 tsp garlic powder

CABBAGE SLAW
1½ cups (105 g) finely shredded cabbage
Juice of 1 lime
Salt and pepper

CHIPOTLE RANCH
½ cup (120 ml) cashew cream (page 93) or vegan mayo
2 tsp (5 g) chipotle powder (see Fresh Tips! for substitutions)
2 tsp (10 ml) lime juice
¼–½ tsp agave or maple syrup
¼ tsp salt

Cut the tofu into 1-inch (2.5-cm)-thick slabs, then put them in single layer on a clean kitchen towel. Cover them with another towel and a cast-iron pan (or something equally as heavy) for 5 minutes.

In a shallow bowl, combine the water, soy sauce, kelp powder and garlic powder. Whisk together. Slice the tofu into nugget-sized pieces. Gently toss the tofu in the marinade until well coated.

Combine the cabbage, lime juice and a sprinkle of salt and pepper. Mix well and set aside.

Make the chipotle ranch. In a small bowl, mix together the cashew cream, chipotle powder, lime juice, agave and salt. Taste and add more lime, salt or agave if desired, then set aside.

BREADING

1 tbsp (8 g) cornstarch or tapioca flour

1 cup (92 g) chickpea or rice flour

1 tbsp (12 g) kelp powder

2 tsp (5 g) garlic powder

2 tsp (5 g) chili powder

2 tsp (4 g) cumin

1½ tsp (9 g) sea salt

FOR FRYING

2 cups (480 ml) oil (see Fresh Tips!)

⅔ cup (160 ml) aquafaba (the liquid from 1 can of chickpeas)

FOR SERVING

8–10 small corn or flour tortillas

2 ripe avocados

¼ small red onion, finely diced

¼ cup (4 g) cilantro, chopped

1 lime, sliced

Make the breading. Sprinkle the cornstarch over the tofu pieces and gently toss to coat. In a shallow bowl, combine the flour, kelp powder, garlic powder, chili powder, cumin and salt in a shallow bowl. Line a plate with paper towels.

Heat the oil in a frying pan over medium-high heat for 2 minutes. Dunk the tofu in aquafaba, then coat the pieces with the flour mixture. Working in batches so you don't overcrowd the pan, fry the tofu until golden brown, about 2 to 3 minutes. Carefully flip and fry for another 2 minutes. When finished, transfer the fried tofu to the paper towels. If your oil is too hot by the second or third batch, reduce the heat slightly.

Warm the tortillas. Dice the avocados. Assemble the tacos with a few pieces of tofu, avocado, cabbage slaw, onion and cilantro. Finish with a squeeze of lime and a generous drizzle of chipotle ranch.

FRESH TIPS!

Any oil with a high smoke point works well for frying, such as grapeseed oil, avocado oil or canola oil.

Use one chipotle pepper in adobo sauce if you can't find chipotle powder. Blend the pepper with the cashew cream, lime juice, agave and salt until smooth and creamy, about 2 minutes.

Use more kelp powder for a deeper seafood flavor. Use less to decrease the seafood flavor.

PORTOBELLO-WALNUT BOLOGNESE

Juicy portobellos and crunchy walnuts make a shockingly satisfying replacement for beef in this rich, flavorful Bolognese. A splash of red wine adds complexity to the simple dish while plenty of herbs and vegan Parmesan build flavor and add richness. The result is seriously delicious and sure to make it into your rotation of easy, weeknight meals.

PREP TIME: 15 MINUTES • COOK TIME: 25 MINUTES • YIELD: 4 SERVINGS

BOLOGNESE SAUCE

3 tbsp (45 ml) olive oil or vegetable broth (see Fresh Tip! for oil-free version)

2 large shallots

8 oz (227 g) portobello mushrooms (about 4 medium caps)

5–7 cloves garlic, minced

2 tbsp (11 g) Italian seasoning, plus more to taste

2 cups (234 g) chopped walnuts

2 tsp (12 g) sea salt, plus more to taste

Pinch of red pepper flakes, plus more to taste

3 tbsp (42 g) tomato paste

1 (28-oz [794-g]) can tomato sauce

¼ cup (60 ml) dry red wine

¼ cup (6 g) basil leaves, tightly packed

FOR SERVING

8 oz (227 g) brown rice or chickpea noodles of choice

½ cup (60 g) shredded vegan Parmesan or mozzarella (optional, store-bought or page 57 and 58)

In a large pan, heat the oil over medium-high heat. Finely dice the shallots, then add them to the pan. Sauté for 1 to 2 minutes. Meanwhile, finely chop the portobello caps.

Add the garlic and Italian seasoning to the pan and cook for 1 minute until fragrant, stirring often so that the garlic doesn't burn. Add the chopped mushrooms, walnuts, sea salt and red pepper flakes. Stir well. Cook until the mushrooms release some of their liquid, about 2 to 3 minutes, stirring occasionally.

Add the tomato paste, tomato sauce and red wine. Stir until well incorporated. Reduce the heat to medium-low. Taste, then adjust the seasoning if desired by adding more salt, Italian seasoning or red pepper flakes. Cover and simmer for 15 minutes to allow the flavors to meld. Add 1 to 2 tablespoons (15 to 30 ml) of water at a time to thin the sauce and deglaze the pan as needed.

While the sauce simmers, cook the pasta in salted water according to package instructions. Rinse, dry and finely chop the basil. Stir the basil into the sauce just before serving. Divide the pasta among the serving bowls and ladle a large scoop of Bolognese over each. Top with vegan Parmesan or mozzarella (if using) and dig in!

FRESH TIP!

To make the oil-free version, preheat a nonstick pan over medium to medium-high heat. Add the shallots and vegetable broth to the hot pan. Sauté for 1 to 2 minutes, then continue the recipe as written above. Add 1 to 2 tablespoons (15 to 30 ml) of broth or pasta water at a time as needed to prevent sticking.

EPIC VEGGIE BURGERS

These savory lentil-walnut patties bring tons of flavor, heartiness and crunch without oil! It's almost too good to be true. The combination of cumin, smoked paprika, BBQ and Worcestershire sauce creates a deep savory flavor, making these burgers irresistible and delicious with any combination of toppings.

PREP TIME: 30 MINUTES • COOK TIME: 30 MINUTES • YIELD: 8 BURGERS

2 tbsp (14 g) ground flaxseed

5 tbsp (75 ml) water

1 red bell pepper

1 portobello mushroom

¼ yellow onion

4–5 cloves garlic, minced

½ cup (30 g) Italian parsley, packed

1½ cups (297 g) cooked brown lentils

1 cup (125 g) chopped walnuts

2 tbsp (30 ml) BBQ sauce

1 tbsp (15 ml) vegan Worcestershire sauce

1 tsp salt

½ tsp cumin

½ tsp smoked paprika

¼–½ tsp red pepper flakes

½ cup (25 g) panko or gluten-free panko breadcrumbs, plus more as needed

2 tbsp (20 g) hemp seeds

FOR SERVING (OPTIONAL)

Burger buns of choice or butter lettuce leaves

1½ cups (375 g) your favorite hummus

Vegan cheese

Sliced tomato

Lettuce

Sliced pickles

Sliced avocado

Sprouts

Preheat the oven to 400°F (204°C). Line a baking sheet with parchment paper.

Whisk together the flaxseed and water in a small bowl. Set aside. Very finely dice the pepper, mushroom and onion. Preheat a nonstick pan over medium heat. When it's hot, scatter the diced vegetables in the pan. Cook the vegetables for 3 to 4 minutes, until some of the liquid has cooked off, stirring often. Add the garlic to the pan for the last 2 minutes. Remove the vegetables from the heat when done.

Chop the parsley in a food processor. Add the lentils, cooked vegetables, walnuts, BBQ sauce, Worcestershire sauce, salt, cumin, paprika and red pepper flakes. Pulse four to five times, then stop to scrape the sides. Pulse a few more times until the paste is well combined but still textured. You want a VERY chunky paste with visible pieces of vegetables and walnuts remaining.

Transfer the mixture to a large bowl. Add the flaxseed "egg," breadcrumbs and hemp seeds. Use a rubber spatula to mix well. Taste, then adjust the spices if desired. If the mixture feels too wet or sticky, add 1 to 2 tablespoons (4 to 8 g) of breadcrumbs at a time. The patties should feel slightly moist but not sticky. If you have time, chill the paste for 10 minutes in the freezer. Form the patties using about a ½ cup (120 g) of paste each, and place them on the baking sheet. Flatten them into discs, about ¾ inch (19 mm) thick.

Bake for 15 minutes, then flip and bake for 15 more minutes. While the patties bake, toast the buns and prepare your toppings! I love mine with hummus. If you're using sliced vegan cheese, place it over the patties for the final 5 minutes of cook time. If you're using homemade Smoky Gouda (page 42), spread it on the toasted bun. Build your burger on a toasted bun and top with hummus, tomato, lettuce, pickles, avocado and sprouts.

FRESH TIP!

The patties hold their shape best when chilled, but you can skip this step if you're pressed for time. The patties can also be frozen before baking. Bake at 400°F (204°C) for about 32 to 35 minutes, until crisp.

MEAL-PREP JACKFRUIT CARNITAS

Once you learn the basic method for preparing jackfruit, any pulled meat dish can be replicated using similar spices. Here, I've created a plant-based carnitas recipe by using traditional seasonings but swapping the pork for jackfruit. The result is so delicious and flavorful, you won't miss the meat at all!

PREP TIME: 20 MINUTES • COOK TIME: 45 MINUTES • YIELD: 4 SERVINGS

2 (20-oz [567-g]) cans jackfruit (in water or brine, not juice)

½ white onion, diced

¾ cup (180 ml) vegetable broth, divided

4 cloves garlic, minced

1 jalapeño, minced

1 tbsp (6 g) ground cumin

1½ tsp (4 g) chili powder (see Fresh Tips!)

1 tbsp (3 g) dried oregano

1½ tsp (9 g) sea salt

½ tsp brown sugar (see Fresh Tips!)

¼ tsp smoked paprika

¾ cup (180 ml) orange juice

2 tbsp (30 ml) olive oil (optional)

1 large avocado

¼ cup (4 g) cilantro or microgreens

½ cup (75 g) small tomatoes

6 cups (1.1 kg) cooked quinoa (see Fresh Tips!)

¼ tsp sea salt

Juice of ½ lime

6 oz (170 g) baby spinach

1 (14-oz [400-g]) can black or pinto beans, drained and rinsed

1 cup (136 g) frozen fire-roasted corn, thawed

½ cup (120 ml) pico de gallo or salsa (see Fresh Tips!)

½ cup (60 g) shredded vegan Cheddar (store-bought or from page 61)

¾ cup (180 ml) yogurt or cashew cream (page 93)

Preheat the oven to 425°F (218°C). Lightly oil a large, nonmetal baking dish. Drain the jackfruit. Trim away the tough core pieces, then use your hands to shred and break apart the jackfruit, discarding the seeds as you go.

Place a large frying pan over medium heat. Add the onion and 1 tablespoon (15 ml) of vegetable broth to the pan. Cook for 1 minute, then add the garlic, jalapeño and 1 tablespoon (15 ml) of broth. Stir well and cook for 1 more minute.

Add the jackfruit and 2 more tablespoons (30 ml) of broth to the pan and stir. Season with the cumin, chili powder, oregano, salt, brown sugar and paprika. Add the orange juice and ½ cup (120 ml) of broth. Increase the heat to medium-high. Cook until the liquid is absorbed, about 5 minutes, stirring often. Add the olive oil (if using) for a richer, crispier texture.

Spread the jackfruit evenly in the baking dish. Bake for 35 minutes, stirring well halfway through.

While the jackfruit cooks, prepare the toppings. Pit and slice the avocado. Chop the cilantro. Slice the tomatoes.

Season the quinoa with salt and lime juice. Divide the quinoa and spinach among your bowls or meal-prep containers. Layer with jackfruit carnitas, beans, corn, tomatoes, pico de gallo, avocado, vegan Cheddar and cilantro or microgreens. Drizzle with yogurt or cashew cream just before serving. If you're making this dish for meal prep, bury the avocado so it doesn't oxidize and change color.

FRESH TIPS!

I recommend using ancho chili powder if you can find it.

You can swap the quinoa for brown rice, and you can use coconut sugar, maple syrup or agave instead of brown sugar.

If you're using salsa instead of pico de gallo, layer it on top just before serving or serve on the side. If you're meal prepping this recipe, you can slice the avocado just before serving rather than burying it in the dish.

SPICY BREAKFAST SAUSAGE MUFFINS

If you've never made vegan breakfast sausage at home, you are missing out! It couldn't be easier, and the end result is ah-mazing! Plenty of herbs and spices, including fennel, thyme, rosemary and sage, provide a special blast of flavor. Fans of sweet and savory should definitely give the maple-chipotle sauce a try!

PREP TIME: 15 MINUTES • COOK TIME: 15 MINUTES • YIELD: 6 SERVINGS

MAPLE-CHIPOTLE AIOLI
1 cup (160 g) raw cashews, soaked for 6+ hours or boiled for 10 minutes

1 canned chipotle pepper

1 tbsp (15 ml) adobo sauce

1 tbsp (15 ml) maple syrup

⅓ cup (80 ml) water

½ tsp salt

½ tsp lemon juice

SPICY BREAKFAST SAUSAGE
1 lb (454 g) vegan ground beef, thawed (see Fresh Tips!)

1 tbsp (2 g) finely chopped fresh sage (see Fresh Tips! for substitutions)

1 tbsp (12 g) light brown sugar

2 tsp (1 g) fresh thyme, finely chopped (see Fresh Tips! for substitutions)

1½ tsp (4 g) fennel seeds

¾ tsp freshly ground black pepper

½ tsp sea salt

½ tsp fresh rosemary, finely chopped (see Fresh Tips! for substitutions)

⅛ tsp nutmeg

⅛–¼ tsp red pepper flakes

FOR SERVING
6 whole-grain or gluten-free English muffins

3 tbsp (42 g) vegan butter

1 cup (125 g) or 6 slices vegan cheese of choice

To make the maple-chipotle aioli, add the pre-soaked cashews, chipotle pepper, adobo sauce, maple syrup, water, salt and lemon juice to a high-speed blender. Blend on high until smooth and creamy, about 2 to 3 minutes. Set aside.

In a medium bowl, mix the vegan ground beef, sage, brown sugar, thyme, fennel seeds, pepper, salt, rosemary, nutmeg and red pepper flakes. Mix well until thoroughly combined.

Put a flat pan over medium heat. Form the sausage mixture into patties. Use a small melon scooper for small patties or an ice cream scooper to make wider patties, depending on the size of your English muffins. Flatten the patties to about ½-inch (12-mm) thickness. Cook until browned, about 2 minutes on each side.

While the sausage cooks, toast and butter the English muffins. Spread your preferred vegan cheese onto the muffins. (I love the Smoky Gouda on page 42!) If using sliced vegan cheese, melt it on the sausage as the second side cooks.

Build the sandwiches on a toasted muffin, with breakfast sausage topped with melted cheese and a dollop of maple-chipotle aioli.

FRESH TIPS!

Swap 1½ teaspoons (2 g) of dried sage, 1 teaspoon of dried thyme and ¼ teaspoon of dried rosemary for fresh ingredients as needed.

Any pea-based vegan ground beef will work in this recipe. If you prefer a whole-food, plant-based version, you can find it on my website: carrotsandflowers.com.

The sausage patties can be frozen prior to cooking. Wrap them well and store in the freezer for up to 2 weeks. Be sure to thaw them in the fridge before cooking.

The canned chipotle peppers can be individually frozen to save for another recipe. I like to keep an ice tray in the freezer for leftover sauces and things like this. Once frozen, I transfer to a labeled container for future use.

MOLE JACKFRUIT TACOS

I could write an entire chapter about my love for mole sauce. It's a savory Mexican sauce made with a hint of cocoa and plenty of spice, perfect for satisfying a sweet and salty craving. By the way, did you know our love for sweet and salty combinations exists because we have taste buds on our tongues that only activate in the presence of these two flavors together? Nature, biology and millions of years of evolution want you to enjoy these vegan mole tacos!

PREP TIME: 15 MINUTES • COOK TIME: 50 MINUTES • YIELD: 12 TACOS

JACKFRUIT

2 (20-oz [567-g]) cans jackfruit (in water or brine, not juice)

1 tbsp (15 ml) grapeseed or other mild oil

1 white onion, diced

5 cloves garlic, minced

2 tbsp (16 g) chili powder

1 tbsp (6 g) cumin

1 tsp sea salt

¼ tsp cayenne (optional)

¾ cup (180 ml) vegetarian chicken broth

MOLE SAUCE

½ cup (100 g) mole paste

½ (14-oz [400-g]) can fire-roasted tomatoes, drained

2 tbsp (14 g) cocoa powder

1 tbsp (12 g) brown sugar

1 tbsp (8 g) chili powder

2 tsp (10 ml) lime juice

1 tsp cinnamon

1 tsp sea salt, plus more to taste

¾ cup (180 ml) vegetarian chicken broth, plus more as needed

FOR SERVING

12 corn tortillas

2 (14-oz [400-g]) cans vegetarian refried black beans

¼ red onion, finely diced

½ cup (8 g) cilantro, chopped

1 cup (240 ml) plain unsweetened cashew yogurt or cashew cream (page 93)

Preheat the oven to 400°F (204°C).

Drain the jackfruit. Trim away the tough core pieces and remove the seeds, then roughly chop the jackfruit. This will help achieve a meaty, pulled texture.

Put a large pan over medium heat. Pour in the oil. Sauté the onion for 1 to 2 minutes, until it becomes slightly translucent. Add the garlic and cook for 1 minute until fragrant. Remove half of the cooked onion and garlic. Set aside for the sauce.

Add the jackfruit to the pan, along with the chili powder, cumin, salt and cayenne (if using). Stir, then add the broth. Reduce the heat slightly and cover. Cook the jackfruit until the liquid is absorbed, about 10 minutes. Remove the lid often to stir and mash the jackfruit pieces until the mixture becomes stringy and resembles pulled pork.

Lightly oil a large, nonmetal baking pan. Spread the jackfruit in the pan in an even layer. Bake for 20 minutes.

While the jackfruit bakes, make the mole sauce. Combine the remaining onions and garlic in a blender with the mole paste, tomatoes, cocoa powder, brown sugar, chili powder, lime juice, cinnamon, salt and the broth. Blend until smooth, about 1 minute. Taste and adjust the seasoning, if desired. Use more broth for a thinner sauce. Traditional mole sauce is the consistency of a thick gravy.

When the jackfruit has baked for 20 minutes, stir in the mole sauce. Mix well and use a fork to shred the jackfruit even more. Bake the jackfruit for another 20 minutes. This second bake time makes it extra meaty and chewy.

Heat the tortillas and beans. Season the beans with a little extra salt, chili powder and lime juice, if desired. Build the tacos in a tortilla with jackfruit, beans, red onion, cilantro and cashew yogurt.

FRESH TIP!

Find mole paste in the Latin American section of most grocery stores. Jackfruit is sold at some grocery stores, health food stores and Indian and Asian markets. Be sure to get jackfruit in brine or water, not juice.

ITALIAN MEATLOAF

This classic meatloaf recipe is a favorite of mine from my pre-vegan days. Filled with Italian spices and herbs and topped with marinara sauce, the only thing that's changed is the beef and eggs, which have been swapped out with vegan ground beef and flax eggs. The end result is a hearty, flavorful meatloaf that no one would guess is made from plants!

PREP TIME: 20 MINUTES • COOK TIME: 45 MINUTES • YIELD: 6 TO 8 SERVINGS

2 tbsp (14 g) ground flaxseed

5 tbsp (75 ml) water

½ red bell pepper

2 shallots

3 cloves garlic

¼ cup (6 g) fresh basil, packed

32 oz (900 g) pea-based ground beef (see Fresh Tips!)

2 tsp (10 ml) vegan Worcestershire sauce

1½ cups (162 g) regular or gluten-free Italian breadcrumbs

1 tbsp (6 g) Italian seasoning

1 tsp red pepper flakes

¾ tsp salt

1½ cups (360 ml) marinara sauce, divided

SUGGESTED SIDES

Mixed green salad

Sautéed broccoli

Preheat the oven to 425°F (218°C). In a large bowl, mix the flaxseed and water. Set aside to thicken.

Very finely dice the red bell pepper and shallots. Make sure the pieces are small, or the meatloaf won't hold together. You can speed this step up by pulsing larger chunks in a food processor instead of dicing by hand.

Lightly oil a pan and place it over medium heat. Let the pepper and shallots cook for a minute while you mince the garlic. Add the garlic to the pan and cook until the peppers are soft, about 5 minutes, stirring occasionally. While the vegetables cook, mince the basil.

Add the peppers, shallots, garlic and basil to the flax mixture, along with the vegan ground beef, Worcestershire sauce, breadcrumbs, Italian seasoning, red pepper flakes and salt. Mix well with your hands until thoroughly combined.

Lightly oil a loaf pan. Press the beef into the pan. Cover the beef with ¾ cup (180 ml) of the marinara sauce and reserve the rest for serving.

Bake for 40 to 45 minutes. Halfway through, poke several holes in the meatloaf with a fork or chopstick. The oils tend to rise to the top of the meatloaf when baking, and this helps keep the meatloaf nice and juicy.

Remove from the oven and let sit for 5 minutes. Warm the reserved marinara. Slice the meatloaf and serve with marinara. Serve with a mixed green salad or sautéed vegetables, if desired.

FRESH TIPS!

Use refrigerated or frozen (and thawed) pea-based vegan ground beef, not crumbles. Beyond Meat and Impossible Foods are popular brands, but many mainstream grocery stores are releasing more affordable pea-based options that cook the same way.

For cheesy meatloaf, mix in ⅓ cup (40 g) of chopped or shredded vegan Parmesan or mozzarella.

CHEESY

UNLOCKING THE SECRETS TO INCREDIBLE VEGAN CHEESE

Cheese lovers, rejoice! I have great news. You can give up dairy without giving up cheese! Truth be told, quality vegan cheese isn't actually that different from dairy cheese, taste-wise. When you break down the elements of a truly delicious cheese, you find characteristics that can be easily achieved with wholesome ingredients, such as nuts, seeds and spices.

Vegan cheese can melt and stretch—just like dairy! It can be sharp and smoky, like farmhouse Cheddar; salty and marinated, like feta; or whipped into a fluffy ricotta. With just a few simple tools and a bit of vegan magic, you can achieve nearly any type of cheese you're craving.

This chapter will walk you through the best, easiest and tastiest ways to make incredible vegan cheeses and cheesy dishes from the comfort of your own kitchen! Start with easy, mouthwatering recipes like my Smoky Gouda Melt (page 42) or Baked Spinach-Artichoke Mac 'n' Cheese (page 41), made with easy-to-find supermarket ingredients.

When you've mastered those, work your way up to more advanced recipes like Sliceable Farmhouse Cheddar (page 61) or Cashew Caprese Mozzarella (page 58), both of which are still quite simple but require a specialty ingredient. No matter where you are in your cheese-making journey, by the end of this chapter, you'll be an expert at crafting a variety of amazing plant-based cheeses at home. Let's kick things off with my most versatile cheese recipe—a customizable 5-minute melty vegan cheese you're going to love!

METHOD

To make melty vegan cheese in 5 minutes, blend the ingredients in a high-speed blender on high until very smooth, about 2 minutes. Pour into a very hot saucepan. Stir and cook, scraping the bottom and sides of the pan. Keep stirring until the cheese is very thick and the lumps are gone, about 3 to 5 minutes. You will be amazed at how stretchy the cheese becomes! Use it for grilled cheese sandwiches, in lasagna or add cooked pasta to make easy vegan mac 'n' cheese! When reheating, lots of heat ensures that the cheese becomes melty again, such as direct contact with a hot pan, time in a hot oven or heating in a microwave.

HOW TO MAKE MELTY VEGAN CHEESE IN 5 MINUTES

CASHEWS

½ cup (80 g) of cashews soaked overnight or boiled to soften

TAPIOCA FLOUR

¼ cup (40 g) to make the cheese stretchy

NUTRITIONAL YEAST

1½ to 2 tablespoons (14 to 17 g) to make it taste cheesy!

SPICES

Totally customizable, but a good base would include 1 teaspoon of onion powder for a mild cheese like mozzarella or 1 teaspoon of smoked paprika for a Cheddar or Gouda.

ACID

½ teaspoon of lemon juice or vinegar for tang

WATER

1½ cups (360 ml)

SALT & PEPPER

¾ teaspoon of salt and ½ teaspoon of pepper. I like using white pepper for mild cheese and red pepper flakes for bold cheese.

GARLIC

1 clove for a mild cheese, 2 cloves for a bold cheese

METHOD

BLEND **POUR AND STIR** **ENJOY!**

BAKED SPINACH-ARTICHOKE MAC 'N' CHEESE

Everyone's favorite party dip gets a main-course makeover! We've got layers of tang thanks to the grilled artichokes and lemon zest, mingling with creamy cashew cheese, crunchy breadcrumbs and perfectly cooked pasta. What are you waiting for? Go make this right now!

PREP TIME: 10 MINUTES • COOK TIME: 15 MINUTES • YIELD: 4 TO 6 SERVINGS

2 tbsp (34 g) salt

2 cups (200 g) brown rice elbows

1 (14-oz [400-g]) jar grilled marinated artichoke hearts

1 (10-oz [283-g]) package frozen spinach, thawed

1 tbsp (15 ml) olive oil

4 cloves garlic, divided

¼ tsp lemon zest

⅛ + ¾ tsp salt, divided

⅛ tsp red pepper flakes

1⅓ cups (320 ml) water

½ cup (80 g) raw cashews, soaked for 6 hours or boiled for 10 minutes

3 tbsp (23 g) tapioca flour

3 tbsp (26 g) nutritional yeast

¼ tsp white pepper

½ tsp lemon juice

½ cup (60 g) shredded vegan Parmesan, divided (see Fresh Tip!)

⅓ cup (37 g) regular or gluten-free breadcrumbs

Preheat the oven to 450°F (232°C). Add 2 tablespoons (34 g) of salt to a medium pot of water. Bring to a boil and cook the brown rice elbows for 1 minute less than package instructions.

Drain and chop the artichoke hearts. Use a clean kitchen towel to squeeze the excess water from the spinach.

In a medium pan, heat the olive oil. Mince 1 clove of garlic and add it to the pan. Cook for 30 seconds, until fragrant, then add the spinach, artichoke hearts and lemon zest. Season with ⅛ teaspoon of salt and the red pepper flakes. Sauté for 2 minutes, until the artichokes begin to brown. Remove from the heat.

Put a saucepan over medium-high heat. While it heats, combine the water, cashews, remaining 3 cloves of garlic, flour, yeast, ¾ teaspoon of salt, white pepper and lemon juice in a high-speed blender. Blend for 2 minutes, until smooth. Transfer the cashew mixture to the hot pan. Begin stirring right away, scraping the bottom and sides of the pan to prevent sticking. When it gets lumpy, stir faster. Continue stirring until the lumps are gone and then add the cooked pasta, spinach-artichoke mixture and ¼ cup (30 g) of the Parmesan. Mix well.

Transfer the pasta to an oiled 9 x 9–inch (23 x 23–cm) glass or ceramic baking dish. Sprinkle the breadcrumbs and remaining Parmesan over the top. Bake for 8 to 10 minutes, until bubbling and crisp, then serve!

FRESH TIP!

This recipe works better with store-bought vegan Parmesan. If using homemade Parmesan (page 57), reduce the amount to ¼ cup (30 g) and sprinkle it on top before baking.

SMOKY GOUDA MELT

You're going to be obsessed with this smoky Gouda cheese melt! The olive oil and spices give this cheese a rich, complex, savory flavor that is SO drool-worthy. Using the 5-minute tapioca method (pages 38–39), this cheese comes together in 5 minutes flat when made with pre-soaked cashews. If you're feeling extra, try this melt on a vegan pretzel bun!

PREP TIME: 10 MINUTES • COOK TIME: 10 MINUTES • YIELD: 6 SERVINGS

SMOKY GOUDA CHEESE

1¼ cups (300 ml) water

½ cup (80 g) raw cashews, soaked for 6+ hours or boiled for 10 minutes

¼ cup (60 ml) extra virgin olive oil

¼ cup (40 g) tapioca flour

3 tbsp (26 g) nutritional yeast

2 tsp (4 g) smoked paprika

¾ + ⅛ tsp sea salt

½ tsp onion powder

½ tsp Dijon mustard

⅛ tsp cayenne

FOR SERVING

2 beefsteak tomatoes

12 slices of bread or 6 pretzel buns

12 slices vegan ham (optional)

6 tbsp (84 g) vegan butter

Pickle, sliced

10 cups (2.5 L) soup of choice

Preheat a saucepan over medium-high heat. Meanwhile, combine the water, cashews, oil, tapioca flour, yeast, paprika, salt, onion powder, Dijon mustard and cayenne in a high-powered blender. Blend on high until smooth and creamy, about 2 minutes.

When the pan is very hot, pour the cheese mixture into it. Begin stirring right away with a wooden spoon. Scrape the bottom and sides of the pan. Stir and scrape constantly for 4 to 5 minutes. The cheese will get lumpy. Continue stirring quickly until all lumps disappear and the cheese is very gooey. Remove from the heat.

Slice the tomatoes, discarding the watery seeds. Assemble the sandwiches with a thick layer of Gouda on your bread or bun. Press the tomato into the cheese and layer the vegan ham on top, if using. Top with bread, then butter the outsides. Put a griddle pan over medium heat.

When the pan is hot, grill the sandwiches until crisp and golden brown, about 2 minutes on each side. Serve right away, ideally with a sliced pickle and cup of soup.

FRESH TIP!

The stretchiness of the tapioca is activated by contact with a very hot pan. Preheating the saucepan before making this cheese is a crucial step. If the saucepan is not hot, the cheese will not get as stretchy. You should hear a loud sizzle when pouring the cashew mixture into the pan.

CHICKEN BROCCOLI ALFREDO MAC 'N' CHEESE

Classic Alfredo seasonings in a creamy cashew cheese sauce are the base of this vegan comfort food mash-up, made extra delicious with the addition of vegan chicken and crunchy broccoli. The combination of savory flavors with creamy and crunchy textures is beyond satisfying.

PREP TIME: 20 MINUTES • COOK TIME: 15 MINUTES • YIELD: 6 SERVINGS

CHICKEN & BROCCOLI PASTA
3 cups (300 g) brown rice elbows

1 tbsp (15 ml) olive oil

1 shallot, finely diced

2 cloves garlic, minced

12 oz (340 g) vegan chicken, chopped

12 oz (340 g) small broccoli florets

ALFREDO SAUCE
1 heaping cup (170 g) raw cashews, soaked for 6+ hours or boiled for 10 minutes

1½ cups (360 ml) water

1 tbsp (15 ml) lemon juice

2 large cloves garlic

3 large sage leaves

2 tsp (4 g) Italian seasoning

2 tbsp (17 g) nutritional yeast

Scant ½ tsp white pepper

¾ tsp salt

2 tbsp (15 g) tapioca flour

FOR SERVING (OPTIONAL)
¼ cup (30 g) shredded vegan Parmesan (store-bought or page 57)

In a medium pot, boil the brown rice elbows in salted water according to package instructions. Heat the oil in a large, deep pan over medium-high heat.

Cook the shallot and garlic for 1 to 2 minutes, then add the vegan chicken and broccoli. Cook until the vegan chicken is crisp and browned and broccoli is bright green and tender, about 5 to 6 minutes.

Make the Alfredo sauce. Add the cashews, water, lemon juice, garlic, sage, Italian seasoning, yeast, white pepper, salt and flour to a high-speed blender. Blend on high until smooth and creamy, about 2 minutes. Drain the pasta in a colander, then immediately put the pot back on medium-high heat.

Pour the cashew mixture into the pot. Stir well, scraping the bottom and sides of the pan, until the sauce is very thick and smooth, about 3 to 4 minutes. Combine the pasta, cheese, broccoli and chicken. Mix well. Divide into serving bowls and top with a sprinkle of vegan Parmesan (if using).

FRESH TIP!

Use pre-breaded vegan chicken strips for a richer flavor and crispier texture. If using, cook separately according to package instructions.

ROASTED VEGETABLE ROMESCO LASAGNA

This romesco sauce is an easy blend of marinara, roasted peppers and cashews. It comes together quickly and takes this lasagna from average to exceptional in just a few minutes, especially when combined with herb-roasted vegetables and creamy tofu ricotta. The ricotta recipe is just as versatile—use it any time you want to add a cheesy dose of protein to your pasta dishes!

PREP TIME: 1 HOUR • COOK TIME: 25 MINUTES • YIELD: 8 SERVINGS

ROMESCO SAUCE

½ red onion, thinly sliced

2 small zucchini, sliced

8 oz (227 g) mushrooms, halved

2 red bell peppers, chopped

½ small eggplant, thinly sliced

2 cups (185 g) broccoli florets, chopped

1 tbsp (15 ml) olive oil

1 tsp Italian seasoning

1 tsp garlic powder

1 tsp sea salt

½ tsp pepper

TOFU RICOTTA

10 oz (283 g) firm tofu

2 tbsp (17 g) nutritional yeast

¾ tsp salt

1 tsp lemon juice

½ tsp garlic powder

¼ tsp pepper

LASAGNA

1½ cups (240 g) raw cashews, soaked for 6+ hours or boiled for 10 minutes

2 (24-oz [680-g]) jars marinara sauce

½ (16-oz [453-g]) package egg-free, no-boil lasagna noodles (see Fresh Tips!)

2 cups (240 g) store-bought vegan mozzarella or Cashew Caprese Mozzarella (page 58)

½ cup (12 g) basil, loosely packed

Preheat the oven to 425°F (218°C). Line two baking sheets with parchment paper. Spread the red onion, zucchini, mushrooms, bell peppers, eggplant and broccoli on the sheets. Drizzle with the olive oil, then season with the Italian seasoning, garlic powder, salt and pepper. Roast for 15 minutes.

Make the tofu ricotta. Drain the tofu. Wrap it in a clean towel and squeeze the water out. Mash well with your hands, about 2 minutes. Add the nutritional yeast, salt, lemon juice, garlic powder and pepper. Mix well.

Remove the vegetables from the oven and reduce the temperature to 320°F (160°C). Put half of the roasted vegetables in a blender. Reserve the rest for the lasagna filling. Add the cashews, marinara and half of the roasted bell peppers to the blender. Blend on high until smooth and creamy. Taste, then season with salt and pepper, if needed.

Lightly oil a 9 x 13–inch (23 x 33–cm) pan. Spread one-third of the sauce in the pan. Add a layer of noodles on top, then add half of the remaining roasted vegetables, half of the tofu ricotta and ⅔ cup (80 g) of the cheese. Repeat, finishing with the remaining sauce and cheese. Cover with foil and bake for 20 minutes. Remove the foil and cook for another 5 to 10 minutes until very bubbly on top.

Let rest for 5 minutes. Chop the basil. Garnish the lasagna with the chopped basil, then slice and serve.

FRESH TIPS!

When layering the sauce, be sure to thoroughly coat the noodles so they become soft in the oven. Check the cooking instructions on your noodles, as the times may vary. When in doubt, follow the package instructions.

If you can't find egg-free, no-boil lasagna noodles, use regular egg-free lasagna noodles. To prepare, boil a large pot of water with 2 tablespoons (34 g) of salt and 1 tablespoon (15 ml) of olive oil. Cook the noodles according to package instructions, then drain. When they are done, place them back in the pot with cool water until ready to use.

RED PEPPER GRILLED CHEESE

Meet your new favorite sandwich: Red Pepper Grilled Cheese on toasty sourdough! The roasted red pepper adds a tanginess and depth of flavor to the homemade cheese that is super tasty and will leave you craving more. The thick sourdough bread complements the sweetness of the peppers and adds a crunchy element that makes me drool just thinking about it. Now, who's hungry?

PREP TIME: 5 MINUTES • COOK TIME: 15 MINUTES • YIELD: 4 TO 6 SANDWICHES

RED PEPPER CHEESE
1½ cups (360 ml) water

½ cup (80 g) raw cashews, soaked for 6+ hours or boiled for 10 minutes

⅓–½ cup (47–70 g) jarred roasted red peppers, drained

¼ cup (40 g) tapioca flour

3 tbsp (26 g) nutritional yeast

2 cloves garlic

1 tsp lemon juice

¾ + ⅛ tsp salt (scant 1 tsp)

¼ tsp red pepper flakes

GRILLED CHEESE
1 crusty sourdough boule or loaf

6 tbsp (84 g) vegan butter

Preheat a saucepan over medium-high heat. Combine the water, cashews, red peppers, flour, yeast, garlic, lemon juice, salt and red pepper flakes in a high-speed blender. Blend on high until smooth, about 1 to 2 minutes.

Pour the cashew mixture into the hot saucepan. Use a wooden spoon or whisk and begin stirring right away, scraping the bottom and sides of the pan, for about 3 to 5 minutes. When the cheese starts looking lumpy, stir faster. Continue stirring and scraping the pan until the lumps are gone and the cheese becomes a gooey mass. Remove from the heat.

Use a bread knife to cut the sourdough into 1-inch (2.5-cm) slices of bread. Preheat a flat pan over medium heat. Build the sandwiches by spreading 3 tablespoons (45 g) of cheese on the inside and 1 tablespoon (14 g) of butter on the outside. Working in two batches, grill the sandwiches on a flat griddle pan over medium-high heat until crispy and golden brown, about 2 minutes on each side. Press the sandwiches into the pan when cooking to flatten them a bit.

Serve immediately, ideally with a cup of tangy tomato-basil soup!

PESTO MAC 'N' CHEESE

What I love most about pesto is how perfectly it pairs with cheese. The savory nutritional yeast, fresh basil and robust olive oil brings out the salty richness in the cheese. Talk about a match made in heaven! A toasty breadcrumb topping adds an irresistible crunch to this creamy, comforting meal. Save time by using a store-bought vegan pesto or using leftover pesto from Pesto Scrambled Tofu (page 78).

PREP TIME: 20 MINUTES • COOK TIME: 15 MINUTES • YIELD: 6 SERVINGS

3½ cups (350 g) dry pasta elbows or shells

BREADCRUMBS
1 tbsp (15 ml) olive oil

1 cup (108 g) regular or gluten-free breadcrumbs

Sea salt

¾ cup (190 g) vegan pesto, divided (store-bought or page 78)

CHEESE SAUCE
1 cup (160 g) raw cashews, soaked for 6+ hours or boiled for 10 minutes

¼ cup (40 g) tapioca flour

3 tbsp (26 g) nutritional yeast

¾ tsp salt

½ tsp chili pepper flakes

½ tsp lemon juice

1 clove garlic

1⅓ cups (320 ml) water

Boil the pasta in salted water according to package instructions, then drain.

Put a small pan over medium heat. Heat the oil and add the breadcrumbs. Sprinkle with sea salt and add 1 to 2 tablespoons (15 to 30 g) of pesto. Mix well, breaking up the pesto with a spoon or whisk. Toast until golden brown, stirring frequently, about 3 to 4 minutes, then set aside.

Preheat a saucepan over medium heat. Combine the cashews, flour, yeast, salt, chili flakes, lemon juice, garlic and water in a high-speed blender. Blend on high until smooth, about 1 to 2 minutes. When the saucepan is very hot, pour the cashew mixture into the pan. Cook and stir until the cheese is very thick and without lumps, scraping the bottom and sides of the pan, about 3 minutes.

Add the cooked pasta to the cheese sauce and mix well.

Use a large spoon to transfer the mac 'n' cheese to a serving dish. Alternate large spoonfuls of mac 'n' cheese with dollops of the remaining pesto. Finally, add dollops of pesto on top, cover with breadcrumbs and serve!

ONE-POT LENTIL-WALNUT BAKED ZITI

Yum, yum, yum! The only thing better than making this hearty, cozy pasta dish is the lack of dishes in the sink when you're finished. Toasty walnuts and lentils add heartiness and crunch while fennel adds a bright, springy flavor to the sauce. To up the protein, swap the ziti for chickpea penne and add vegan sausage.

PREP TIME: 5 MINUTES • COOK TIME: 35 MINUTES • YIELD: 4 TO 6 SERVINGS

1 tsp olive oil

2 cups (396 g) cooked brown lentils

1 cup (125 g) chopped walnuts

2 vegan Italian sausage links (optional, see Fresh Tips!)

5–6 cloves garlic, minced

½ tsp crushed red pepper flakes

1 (14-oz [400-g]) can diced tomatoes

1 cup (240 ml) tomato sauce

1 tbsp (3 g) dried oregano leaves

1 tsp ground fennel

1 tsp salt, plus more to taste

3 cups (720 ml) water, plus more if needed

12 oz (340 g) ziti pasta (or similar pasta)

½ cup (10 g) fresh basil leaves

½ cup (120 ml) cashew cream (page 93)

½ cup (60 g) vegan Parmesan (store-bought or page 57)

Pepper, to taste

2 tbsp (17 g) nutritional yeast

1 cup (120 g) vegan mozzarella or Cashew Caprese Mozzarella (page 58)

Preheat the oven to 500°F (260°C). Pour the oil in a large, deep, oven-safe pot over medium heat. Add the lentils, walnuts and sausage (if using). Cook until browned, about 3 to 5 minutes.

Add the garlic and red pepper flakes to the pot and cook for 1 to 2 minutes. Add the diced tomatoes, tomato sauce, oregano, fennel and salt. Stir well. Reduce the heat and simmer for 5 to 10 minutes, stirring occasionally.

Add the 3 cups (720 ml) of water and dry pasta to the pot. Bring to a boil, then reduce the heat to a low boil, cover and cook for 10 to 15 minutes, or until the noodles are tender. Remove the cover occasionally to stir. Meanwhile, chiffonade the basil.

Mix in the cashew cream and Parmesan cheese. If the sauce boils down too quickly, add more water ¼ cup (60 ml) at a time to thin. Season with salt and pepper to taste and add the nutritional yeast. Sprinkle the mozzarella evenly over the top. Bake the ziti until the cheese is melty and browned, about 5 to 10 minutes. Top with basil and serve.

FRESH TIPS!

If using pea-based Italian sausage, remove the casing first and crumble it into the pan with the lentils and nuts. Otherwise, finely dice the sausage links.

For a higher protein dish, swap the ziti for chickpea penne.

SECRETLY HEALTHY VEGAN NACHOS

The only thing better than a mouthwatering, heaping plate of nachos is one that is actually good for you! Cooked potato and carrots lighten up this cashew-based cheese, which gets its smoky heat from smoked paprika, chipotle powder and salsa. Make the nachos with Portobello-Walnut "Chorizo" (page 123) or use soy chorizo to save time. For a lighter option, use baked tortilla chips or try this recipe with jicama chips.

PREP TIME: 25 MINUTES • COOK TIME: 15 MINUTES
YIELD: 4 SERVINGS WITH EXTRA QUESO

QUESO

1 large gold potato, diced

1 medium carrot, diced

⅔ cup (105 g) cashews

¾ cup (180 ml) red salsa

½ cup (40 g) nutritional yeast

2 cloves garlic

½ tsp smoked paprika

½ tsp salt

½ tsp chipotle or chili powder

NACHOS

2 large tomatoes or 1 cup (240 g) pico de gallo

1 avocado or ½ cup (117 g) guacamole

Handful of cilantro

1 jalapeño

1 lime

2 cups (520 g) ground vegan chorizo (store-bought or page 123)

1 cup (172 g) canned black beans

½ tsp cumin, plus more to season

¼ tsp salt, plus more to season

1 tsp lime juice

10 oz (283 g) tortilla chips or 2 large jicamas

¼ cup (18 g) shredded purple cabbage (optional)

¼ cup (60 ml) cashew cream (page 93) or cashew yogurt

Boil the potato, carrot and cashews until the vegetables are fork-tender, then drain.

While the vegetables are cooking, prepare the toppings. Chop the tomatoes, discarding the watery seeds. If using pico de gallo, drain the excess liquid. Slice the avocado and finely chop the cilantro. Deseed and thinly slice the jalapeño. Slice the lime into wedges. Warm the chorizo. Season the beans with cumin, salt and lime juice, then heat them up.

Combine the potato, carrot, cashews, salsa, yeast, garlic, paprika, salt and chipotle powder in a blender. Blend until smooth, creamy and hot, about 3 to 4 minutes. Stop to scrape down the sides as needed.

Taste the queso and adjust the seasoning, if desired. You can add nutritional yeast for cheesiness, paprika for smokiness, chipotle powder for spice, lime juice for tang or a dash of salt to enhance the flavors. I like my queso very thick, but you can add a little more salsa or water if you want to thin it out.

If using jicama, peel, then slice it into ¼-inch (6-mm) chips. Season them with a teensy sprinkle of salt and cumin. Arrange the tortilla chips or jicama chips on serving plates. Pour the queso over the chips, then top with beans, chorizo, tomatoes, avocado, cilantro and shredded cabbage. Finish with jalapeño slices and serve with a drizzle of cashew cream and lime wedges.

ROASTED GARLIC SUPERFOOD PARMESAN

This roasted garlic Parmesan is simply addictive! Processed nuts and seeds create a texture similar to grated Parmesan. Nutritional yeast and roasted garlic create a flavor profile that's so savory and delicious, you'll want to sprinkle it on pasta, salads and everything in between. Swap some of the brazil nuts and pistachios for sunflower seeds or more pumpkin seeds for a wallet-friendly version. Walnuts and cashews can also be used. Make it your own!

PREP TIME: 5 MINUTES • COOK TIME: 40 MINUTES • YIELD: 1 ⅔ CUPS (240 G)

1 bulb garlic
1 tsp olive oil
⅓ cup (40 g) pumpkin seeds
⅓ cup (43 g) brazil nuts
⅓ cup (40 g) almonds
⅓ cup (35 g) pistachios
1 tsp salt
1 tsp lemon juice
⅓ cup (50 g) nutritional yeast

Preheat the oven to 425°F (218°C). Slice the top off the garlic bulb. Drizzle the garlic with the olive oil. Wrap it with foil. Roast the garlic for 40 minutes. Allow it to cool slightly, then squeeze the cloves from the bulb. Use a towel so you don't burn your hands.

Place the garlic in a food processor, along with the pumpkin seeds, brazil nuts, almonds and pistachios. Process to a coarse grain, similar to grated Parmesan. Add the salt, lemon juice and nutritional yeast. Process again just until combined. Use it on pasta, pizza, salads or wherever you'd like a cheesy superfood sprinkle.

Roasted Garlic Superfood Parmesan keeps in a closed container in the fridge for up to 2 weeks.

CASHEW CAPRESE MOZZARELLA

The secret ingredient to this vegan caprese cheese is kappa carrageenan, a seaweed extract that makes the cheese firm but meltable. The sauerkraut brine adds a hint of fermentation and tang while tasting milder than lemon juice or vinegar. See Fresh Tips! for a version made without kappa carrageenan!

PREP TIME: 15 MINUTES • COOK TIME: 5 MINUTES • YIELD: 8 SERVINGS

Cooking spray

1 cup (160 g) pre-soaked cashews (see Fresh Tips! for options)

2 tbsp (30 ml) sauerkraut brine

2 cloves garlic

2 tbsp (15 g) tapioca flour

¾ tsp salt

½ tsp white pepper

⅛ tsp onion powder

1½ tbsp (13 g) nutritional yeast

⅓ cup (80 ml) melted coconut oil (refined and flavorless)

1⅔ cups (400 ml) water

1 tbsp (2 g) kappa carrageenan (see Fresh Tips!)

Line a rimmed plate with parchment paper and spray it with cooking oil. Put the cashews, brine, garlic, flour, salt, pepper, onion powder, yeast, coconut oil and water in a high-speed blender. Blend until very smooth, about 3 minutes. Stop to scrape down the sides as needed.

Add the kappa carrageenan to the blender. Blend on low until combined, about 30 seconds. Preheat a saucepan over medium-high heat. When it is hot, pour the cashew mixture into the pan. Cook for 4 to 5 minutes, stirring vigorously and continuously, until the mixture is very bubbly.

Transfer the mixture to the rimmed plate. Work quickly, because the kappa carrageenan will set the cheese rapidly as it cools to room temperature. The cheese will firm to a soft but solid texture in 30 minutes to an hour. Once set, invert the cheese onto a cutting board lined with parchment paper. Slice into circles with a round biscuit cutter. Finely chop the remaining pieces to use in sandwiches or quesadillas. The circles are excellent for caprese salads, on pizzas or with crackers as part of a cheese plate. Cover the cheese securely and store it in the fridge. The mozzarella tastes best within 3 to 4 days.

FRESH TIPS!

Soak the cashews for 6 hours or overnight to soften, then drain. You can also boil them for 10 minutes prior to cooking if you're in a hurry. I like to keep pre-soaked nuts in the freezer for convenience. No need to thaw before use!

Kappa carrageenan is most easily found online. It's activated by heat, which is why it should always be incorporated at a low speed. Do not overmix or overheat in the blender or the cheese will not set properly.

TAPIOCA VERSION—Replace the kappa carrageenan with an additional 2 tablespoons (15 g) of tapioca flour. If using this method, preheat the saucepan for 2 minutes before adding the cheese mixture. The tapioca version needs to be chilled for at least 6 hours or overnight before it is firm enough to cut with biscuit cutters.

SLICEABLE FARMHOUSE CHEDDAR

Because it's firm when chilled and melts to a liquid when hot, coconut oil is a key ingredient in making sliceable, vegan cheese that melts. Be sure to look for a coconut oil that advertises as completely flavorless, not just refined. Even a mild coconut flavor will leave an aftertaste. Nutiva is a great brand to look out for. It can be found in most health food stores and some grocery stores.

PREP TIME: 10 MINUTES • COOK TIME: 5 MINUTES • YIELD: 16 SERVINGS

1 cup (160 g) raw cashews, soaked for 6+ hours or boiled for 10 minutes

½ cup (80 g) nutritional yeast

¼ cup (40 g) tapioca flour

2 tbsp (28 g) tomato paste

3 tbsp (50 g) white miso paste

3 cloves garlic

1¼ tsp (3 g) smoked paprika

1⅛ tsp (7 g) sea salt

¼–½ tsp red pepper flakes, or to taste

¾ tsp apple cider vinegar

½ cup (120 ml) melted coconut oil (refined and flavorless)

1⅔ cups (400 ml) filtered water

2 tbsp (4 g) kappa carrageenan (see Fresh Tips! for substitutions)

TAPIOCA VERSION—If you can't find kappa carrageenan, replace it with an additional 2 tablespoons (15 g) of tapioca flour. If using this method, preheat the saucepan for 2 minutes before adding the cheese mixture. The cheese won't be firm enough to shred, but it will still be very delicious and meltable.

Line a small loaf pan or your desired container with parchment paper and a little oil. You can also line it with cling wrap.

Combine the cashews, yeast, flour, tomato paste, miso, garlic, paprika, salt, red pepper flakes, vinegar, oil and water in a high-speed blender. Blend on high until smooth and creamy, about 4 to 5 minutes. Move the tamper continuously as needed to blend. Stop to scrape down the sides often. Once the mixture is very smooth, add the kappa carrageenan and blend on low for another 20 seconds until thoroughly mixed.

Transfer the cheese mixture to a saucepan over medium-high heat. As the cheese heats up, use a wooden spoon or whisk to vigorously stir the cheese, scraping the bottom and sides of the pan. Stir for 3 to 4 minutes, until the mixture begins to bubble a lot. Keep stirring as it tries to boil, about 1 minute. Getting it nice and hot activates the kappa carrageenan, which will set the cheese.

Transfer the mixture to your lined container. Work quickly if you used kappa carrageenan, because the cheese will set quickly as it cools to room temperature. The cheese will set as it cools, in about 30 minutes.

When the cheese is set, gently run a paring knife around the edges to free the cheese. Slice or shred as needed after the cheese is firm. The cheese will keep in a closed container in the fridge for up to 5 days.

FRESH TIPS!

If you live in the United States, do not attempt this recipe using the triple filtered coconut oil from Trader Joe's. It has a faint coconut flavor that does not work well in this recipe.

Kappa carrageenan is most easily found online. It's activated by heat, which is why it should always be incorporated at a low speed. Do not overmix or overheat in the blender or the cheese will not set properly.

MARINATED BAKED ALMOND FETA

Slivered almonds are an ideal choice to make almond cheese because they are already peeled and steamed, so there's no need to soak or boil to soften them, unlike most plant-based cheese recipes. Olive oil and brine add layers of salty flavor while garlic herb olive oil infuses the cheese with even more Mediterranean flavors. Make a batch to enjoy in Meatball Gyros (page 16), Tomato Jam and Avocado Tartine (page 90) or Strawberry Bistro Salad (page 109).

PREP TIME: 10 MINUTES • COOK TIME: 20 TO 30 MINUTES, PLUS OVERNIGHT MARINADE
YIELD: 8 TO 10 SERVINGS

ALMOND FETA
2 cups (220 g) slivered almonds

½ cup (120 ml) filtered water

⅓ cup (80 ml) lemon juice

⅓ cup (80 ml) olive oil

1 tbsp (15 ml) olive brine or caper brine

2–3 cloves garlic

1 tsp salt

MARINADE
1 cup (240 ml) sunflower oil

1 tbsp (12 g) peppercorns or 1 tsp cracked pepper

1½ tsp (2 g) dried oregano

5 sprigs thyme

1 clove garlic, smashed and roughly chopped

3 bay leaves

½ cup (120 ml) quality extra virgin olive oil

Preheat the oven to 325°F (163°C). Line a 6- or 8-inch (15- or 20-cm) ceramic or glass baking dish with parchment paper and lightly oil the sides.

Combine the almonds, water, lemon juice, olive oil, olive brine, garlic and salt in a high-speed blender. Blend until you have a very smooth, thick paste. This will take several minutes. Stop to scrape down the sides as needed and use the tamper to evenly blend the cheese. If your blender sounds overworked, stop to give it a 30-second break so it doesn't overheat. You can also add a teensy bit more water to more easily blend the cheese. If you do this, you'll need to transfer the mixture to a cheesecloth and squeeze the water out before continuing.

Transfer the cheese to the lined baking dish. Use your hands to press the cheese into a thin even layer about ½ inch (12 mm) thick. Bake for 20 to 30 minutes, until firm. Bake for 20 minutes for a creamier, more crumbly cheese, if you plan to skip the marinating step. Bake for 30 minutes for a very firm cheese that can be diced.

While the cheese bakes, make the marinade. Combine the sunflower oil, peppercorns, oregano, thyme, garlic and bay leaves in a saucepan over medium-low heat. Allow the mixture to bubble, then remove from the heat and add the olive oil. Transfer the mixture to a jar with a lid.

Let the cheese cool, then dice it into cubes. Add the feta cubes to the oil to marinate for 12 hours or overnight in the fridge. Store the cheese in the marinade for up to 2 weeks in the fridge. The oil will become thick after a few days. When this occurs, thaw on the counter for an hour before using.

CULTURED SUNFLOWER GOAT CHEESE

Guess what? You can make fancy, cultured vegan cheese at home with little more than pre-soaked seeds and a few spoonfuls of vegan yogurt! I love using sunflower seeds in this recipe for the earthy undertones, but pre-soaked cashews will also work well. The result is salty and tangy, with a soft, creamy texture reminiscent of goat cheese.

PREP TIME: 15 MINUTES • COOK TIME: 24 TO 48 HOURS • YIELD: 8 TO 10 SERVINGS

2 cups (268 g) sunflower seeds, soaked or boiled (see Fresh Tip! for options)

2 tbsp (30 ml) lemon juice

1 tbsp (15 ml) filtered water

1 small clove garlic

2 tbsp (30 ml) plain unsweetened non-dairy yogurt (any kind except coconut)

Scant 1 tsp sea salt

FOR SERVING

3 tbsp (10 g) minced dill

Crackers

Grapes

FRESH TIP!

Soak the sunflower seeds overnight, then drain. To save time, you can boil them for 15 minutes to soften, then drain and rinse with cool water.

Prepare a clean, dry glass or other nonmetal container. Pour boiling water over the container and lid to sterilize it, then dry with clean paper towels.

Put the sunflower seeds in a high-speed blender or food processor, along with the lemon juice, water and garlic. Blend until very smooth. This will take several minutes. Stop to scrape down the sides often. If you must add more water to assist in blending, use 1 tablespoon (15 ml) at a time, up to 2 or 3 tablespoons (30 to 45 ml). Keep in mind that the more liquid you add, the more whipped and spreadable the cheese will be. For a firmer goat cheese texture, use very little to no water. This process is easier in a food processor, but the blender makes for a creamier cheese.

If the mixture is very warm, put the blender container in the freezer for 5 minutes to cool. If the mixture is too warm, it can affect the bacteria in the yogurt that cultures the cheese. Add the yogurt and salt. Blend on low to medium speed until combined.

Transfer the mixture to the sterilized container. Cover tightly with a paper towel or cheesecloth and rubber band. Let the cheese sit out at room temperature for 24 hours. Afterward, taste with a clean utensil. For a tangier cheese, culture for another 12 to 24 hours. Keep in mind, the cheese will culture more quickly in warmer climates and more slowly in cooler climates.

When the cheese reaches your desired flavor, line a cutting board with cling wrap or parchment paper. Transfer the cheese onto the cutting board. Cover the cheese and use the cling wrap or paper to shape the cheese into a log. Wrap the cheese log and smooth it out using the paper or film. If your cheese is very soft, wrap it in double or triple layered cheesecloth and place it in the fridge for 1 to 2 days until more firm.

Once formed into a log, this cheese looks beautiful covered with minced fresh dill. Simply unwrap the cheese log and coat the outside with the herbs. Serve with crackers and fruit as part of a cheese board.

Store in the refrigerator for up to 5 days. Use on salads, sandwiches, scrambles or wherever you'd like a pop of tangy cheese.

SAVORY

VEGAN UMAMI ESSENTIALS

NUTRITIONAL YEAST

Undeniably an all-star in vegan cuisine. I use it in nearly every cheese recipe and in many sauces for a boost of cheesy, umami flavor. This large, flaked yeast is inactive, meaning it's not the type that makes bread rise. Use 2 tablespoons (17 g) in a mild cheese recipe or up to ½ cup (80 g) for a boldly flavored cheese, like vegan queso (page 54).

SOY SAUCE AND TAMARI

These salty, fermented soybean sauces are vegan pantry staples if there ever was one. Use one or the other to add a savory element to a variety of vegan recipes like bacon, frittatas, stir-fries and more! Tamari is less salty, slightly thicker and is usually gluten-free. Soy sauce is thinner and saltier. I typically prefer tamari or low-sodium soy sauce.

MISO PASTE

Made from fermented soybeans, miso has a complex, salty and savory flavor that enhances everything, from sauces to marinades, stir-fries to vegan cheese. Find it in the refrigerated section, often near the tofu and meat alternatives.

A CRASH COURSE IN PLANT-BASED UMAMI FLAVORS

This chapter is dedicated to melt-in-your-mouth meals and savory vegan breakfasts. It's chock-full of delicious recipes, like BBQ Chicken Pizza (page 81); satisfying eggy dishes like Plantain-Crusted Tofu Benny (page 77); hearty soups, including White Bean Chicken Chili (page 68) and everything in between! But first, let's go over the basics of vegan umami cooking.

Umami—also referred to as savory—is the fifth flavor our taste receptors can detect, along with salty, sour, bitter and sweet. Umami is experienced as a burst of flavor that spreads across your mouth, making it one of the most pleasurable aspects of enjoying a meal. While umami flavors are typically achieved with cultured cheeses, briny fish and salty meats, there are many delicious ways to enjoy the savory foods you crave with vegan ingredients. Allow me to introduce a few of my faves!

MUSHROOMS

The earthiness of mushrooms is a fantastic way to create umami flavors. Use shiitake mushrooms when going for a stronger, sea flavor. Use dried mushrooms to make sauces and broths. My all-time favorite is a jar of quality truffle oil, preferably one that includes real truffle mushrooms.

KALA NAMAK

A.k.a. Indian black salt—a variety of salt that is high in sulfur, which gives it a distinct eggy flavor. A little goes a long way when making Breakfast Burritos (page 70) and Frittata Muffins (page 73). Find this online or in Indian markets. One bag will keep in the pantry for over a year.

SEAWEED

A great way to invoke the salty, ocean flavors of seafood. I often use kelp powder, dulse flakes or a finely ground sheet of nori in recipes like Crispy Tofu Fish Tacos (page 24) and Classic British Fish 'n' Chips (page 20).

OLIVES

Olives add a salty richness and depth to every dish they're in. Make them into a spread, add a few to a salad or simply enjoy a few on the side of your bowl or hummus plate. Save the brine to enhance salty vegan cheeses.

WHITE BEAN CHICKEN CHILI

This flavorful chili is also a lesson in how to make creamy soups without dairy. You will be amazed by how easy it is! Here, we use cashew cream for creaminess and pureed beans to thicken the chili while the corn and zucchini keep the meal nice and light. This is one of my most loved childhood meals. I hope it becomes one of your family favorites too!

PREP TIME: 20 MINUTES • COOK TIME: 25 MINUTES • YIELD: 4 SERVINGS

1 jalapeño

½ white or yellow onion

12 oz (340 g) prepared vegan chicken strips (see Fresh Tip! for substitutions)

1 tbsp (15 ml) olive oil or ¼ cup (60 ml) vegetarian chicken broth

1 (4-oz [113-g]) can green chilis, drained

3 cloves garlic, minced

2 tsp (4 g) cumin

1 tsp chili powder

1 tsp oregano

1 tsp salt

⅛ tsp cayenne

2 small zucchini

2 (14-oz [400-g]) cans white beans, drained, rinsed and divided

3 cups (720 ml) vegan chicken broth, divided

½ cup (68 g) fresh or frozen corn

¼ cup (40 g) raw cashews, soaked for 6+ hours or boiled for 10 minutes

1½ tsp (7 ml) lime juice

FOR SERVING

1 cup (120 g) shredded vegan mozzarella or Cheddar

2 avocados, diced

¼ cup (4 g) cilantro, chopped

¼ cup (60 ml) vegan sour cream or cashew cream (page 93)

10 oz (283 g) tortilla chips

1 lime, cut into wedges

Slice the jalapeño in half width-wise. Deseed then mince half of it. Thinly slice the other half and set aside for garnish. Dice the onion and the vegan chicken. Preheat a pan over medium-high heat. When it's hot, add the oil, onion, green chilis and minced jalapeño. Sauté for 2 to 3 minutes, until the onion is softened.

Add the vegan chicken, garlic, cumin, chili powder, oregano, salt and cayenne. Mix well and cook until the chicken is slightly browned, about 2 to 3 minutes. Slice the zucchini into ¼-inch (6-mm) half moons, then add them to the pan. Mix well and cook for another 3 to 4 minutes, stirring occasionally.

Set aside 1 cup (262 g) of beans and ¼ cup (60 ml) of broth. Add the remaining beans, broth and corn to the pot. Mix well and bring to a simmer. Simmer for 8 to 10 minutes until the zucchini is softened. Meanwhile, in a high-speed blender, blend the reserved beans, broth and cashews on high until smooth and creamy, about 1 minute. Stir the mixture into the soup to thicken. Add the lime juice. Taste and adjust the spices, if desired.

Simmer for another 5 minutes to allow the flavors to mingle, then ladle the chili into serving bowls. Top with shredded cheese, avocado, cilantro, reserved sliced jalapeños and a dollop of sour cream. Serve with tortilla chips and lime wedges.

FRESH TIP!

For a whole-food, plant-based version, swap the vegan chicken for a can of chickpeas or extra corn, zucchini and white beans. Use vegetable broth in place of vegan chicken broth if needed.

BREAKFAST BURRITOS WITH EGGY TOFU SCRAMBLE

Kala namak—a.k.a. Indian black salt—is a type of salt with a high sulfur content. It's basically the holy grail when it comes to making plant-based food taste like eggs. You can find it online, and one bag will last you more than a year. Make a double batch of this tofu scramble for No-Huevos Rancheros (page 86)!

See photo on page 6.

PREP TIME: 20 MINUTES • COOK TIME: 25 MINUTES • YIELD: 4 SERVINGS

10 oz (283 g) firm tofu

CRISPY ROASTED POTATOES

1 lb (454 g) gold potatoes, diced into 1-inch (2.5-cm) pieces

2 bell peppers, diced into 1-inch (2.5-cm) pieces

Cooking spray

½ tsp smoked paprika

½ tsp garlic powder

¼ tsp sea salt

¼ tsp pepper

TOFU SCRAMBLE MARINADE

3 tbsp (45 ml) water

4 tsp (12 g) nutritional yeast

2 tsp (10 ml) lemon juice

1 tsp garlic powder

¾ tsp smoked paprika

¾ tsp turmeric

½ tsp onion powder

½ tsp white pepper

¾ tsp Indian black salt (kala namak)

¼ tsp sea salt

Preheat the oven to 425°F (218°C) and line a baking sheet with parchment paper. Drain the tofu. Cut it into 1-inch (2.5-cm) slabs. Place in a single layer on a clean kitchen towel. Cover with another towel and place a heavy pan on top. Press for 5 minutes.

Put the potatoes and bell peppers on the baking sheet. Spray the potatoes and bell peppers with cooking oil, then toss with paprika, garlic powder, sea salt and pepper until evenly coated. Bake for 25 minutes, turning halfway through.

Meanwhile, make the tofu marinade. In a shallow bowl, combine the water, yeast, lemon juice, garlic powder, paprika, turmeric, onion powder, pepper, black salt and sea salt.

Dice the tofu into cubes (I prefer it like this) or crumble the tofu into 2-inch (5-cm) pieces for a more traditional scramble. Gently toss the tofu in the marinade. Set aside for 10 minutes.

Cooking spray

¼ small white onion, finely diced

2 cloves garlic, minced

FOR SERVING

4 large flour tortillas

1 cup (240 ml) salsa

1 avocado, diced

½ cup (60 g) vegan bacon bits
(optional, for crunch, store-bought or
see Fresh Tip! for recipe)

Hot sauce

Put a pan over medium heat. Spray it with cooking oil and add the onion. Sauté for 1 to 2 minutes. Add the garlic. Stir well and cook for another minute. Push the onions and garlic to the edges of the pan.

Spray the center with cooking oil and add the tofu. Let it cook for 2 to 3 minutes undisturbed (this helps keep it from sticking to the pan), then flip and incorporate the onion and garlic. Cook until golden brown, about 4 to 5 minutes.

Warm the tortillas. Build the burritos with a spoonful of potatoes, a spoonful of tofu, salsa, avocado and a handful of bacon bits. Add a drizzle of hot sauce. Wrap the burritos up tight and grill them on a griddle pan over medium heat until crispy and golden brown, about 2 minutes on each side. Serve with hot sauce and salsa on the side.

FRESH TIP!

In place of store-bought vegan bacon bits, try this recipe!

TEMPEH BACON BITS—Finely chop 10 ounces (283 g) of tempeh into bits. In a shallow bowl, combine 3 tablespoons (45 ml) of tamari, 2 tablespoons (30 ml) of maple syrup, 2 teaspoons (10 ml) of red hot sauce and 2 teaspoons (10 ml) of liquid smoke. Add the tempeh to the marinade and mix. Set aside for 15 minutes. Melt 1 tablespoon (13 g) of coconut oil in a pan over medium heat. Cook the tempeh for 10 to 12 minutes, stirring occasionally, until blackened and sticky.

SUPERGREEN MEAL-PREP FRITTATA MUFFINS

Finally—a savory vegan breakfast option that you can grab and go that isn't basic avocado toast. These flavorful frittata muffins are perfect to fuel you on your busiest day. They're packed with protein, fiber and greens and taste deceptively eggy thanks to the addition of kala namak—a.k.a. Indian black salt.

PREP TIME: 15 MINUTES • COOK TIME: 30 MINUTES • YIELD: 8 FRITTATA MUFFINS

5 tsp (25 ml) olive oil, divided

5 stalks green onion, thinly sliced

3 cloves garlic, minced

2 cups (185 g) broccoli, finely chopped

¼ cup (37 g) frozen spinach, thawed

¼ tsp salt

¼ tsp black pepper

14 oz (400 g) firm tofu

2 tbsp (17 g) nutritional yeast

1 tbsp (15 ml) tamari or soy sauce

1 tbsp (8 g) cornstarch

1 tsp smoked paprika

½ tsp white pepper

½ tsp turmeric

¼ tsp Indian black salt (kala namak)

½ tsp Dijon mustard

½ cup (60 g) shredded vegan Cheddar (store-bought or from page 61)

Preheat the oven to 375°F (191°C). Line a muffin tin with eight cupcake liners. If you don't have cupcake liners, generously spray eight holes of a muffin tin with cooking oil and line the bottoms with tiny circles of parchment paper.

Add 2 teaspoons (10 ml) of oil to a pan. Sauté the green onions for 1 minute, then add the garlic. Cook and stir for 30 seconds until fragrant, then add the broccoli, spinach, salt and black pepper. Cook until the broccoli turns bright green and the spinach is wilted, about 1 minute.

Squeeze the water from the tofu with a clean kitchen towel. In a high-speed blender or food processor, combine the tofu, nutritional yeast, tamari, 1 tablespoon (15 ml) of olive oil, cornstarch, paprika, white pepper, turmeric, black salt and Dijon. Blend to a smooth paste, stopping to scrape down the sides as needed.

Transfer the tofu mixture to a medium bowl. Stir in the cooked vegetables and cheese. You can also do this part in the blender to save dishes. Then spoon the mixture evenly into the muffin tin liners. Smooth out the tops.

Bake for 25 to 30 minutes, or until a toothpick comes out clean. They can be eaten right away, although they taste better when they've had a chance to cool and set. They are best served at room temperature or warm, not hot. Eat the frittata muffins on the go or serve with your choice of sides for a hearty, healthy brunch.

FRESH TIPS!

Store in a closed container in the fridge for up to 4 days. To reheat, bake at 350°F (177°C) for 12 to 14 minutes until heated through. You can also microwave for 1 to 2 minutes, but the texture will be slightly softer.

If you'd like to freeze your frittata muffins, wait until they are completely cool, then wrap well and freeze for up to 2 months. They taste best when thawed in the fridge before reheating.

BAKED TOFU CLUB SANDWICHES

Seasoned nut butter makes a surprisingly delicious "breaded" coating for baked tofu—minus the flour.
The soy drizzled over the tofu adds more flavor while the starch helps the nut butter stick. Once you try it,
you will be obsessed with this easy method—guaranteed!

PREP TIME: 15 MINUTES • COOK TIME: 20 MINUTES • YIELD: 4 SERVINGS

12 oz (340 g) extra-firm tofu

¼ cup (65 g) cashew butter (see Fresh
Tips! for substitutions)

⅓ cup (80 ml) water

1 tsp garlic powder

1 tbsp (9 g) nutritional yeast

2 tsp (4 g) Italian seasoning

1 tsp lemon juice

½ tsp onion powder

Scant ½ tsp salt

¼ tsp pepper

1 tbsp (15 ml) soy sauce or tamari

1 tbsp (8 g) cornstarch or tapioca flour

FOR SERVING

2 large ripe tomatoes

8 large Bibb or green lettuce leaves

8–12 slices vegan brown bread,
sourdough or gluten-free bread

4 tbsp (60 ml) vegan mayo or cashew
cream (page 93)

12 oz (340 g) cooked vegan bacon
(store-bought or page 136)

Preheat the oven to 425°F (218°C). Line a baking sheet with parchment paper.

Slice the tofu into ½-inch (12-mm)-thick slabs. Line the tofu in a single layer on top of a clean kitchen towel. Cover with another towel and place something very heavy—ideally a cast-iron pan—on top.

In a shallow bowl, combine the cashew butter, water, garlic powder, yeast, Italian seasoning, lemon juice, onion powder, salt and pepper. Mix well to combine. It will be very thick.

Unwrap the tofu. Using your fingers or a pastry brush, gently rub the soy sauce into the tofu. Sprinkle half of the cornstarch on the tofu. Gently rub it in, then flip and rub the remaining starch on the other side.

Coat the tofu with the cashew butter mixture. You want a nice thick layer. Place it on the lined baking sheet. Smooth out the cashew layer if needed.

Bake for 10 minutes, then flip and bake for another 8 to 10 minutes, until browned and crisp. Meanwhile, slice the tomato. Wash and dry the lettuce. Toast the bread. Spread a thin layer of mayo on each slice of bread.

Assemble the sandwiches using 3 slices of toasted bread with mayo on each, baked tofu, lettuce, tomato and vegan bacon. Pin with toothpicks and slice into quarters to serve as a club-style sandwich.

FRESH TIPS!

You can use unsweetened almond or sunflower seed butter in place of cashew butter as needed or in case of allergies.

MEDITERRANEAN VERSION—Use pumpernickel or olive bread. Omit the vegan bacon. Layer the tofu with ⅓ cup (90 g) of olive tapenade, 2 sliced tomatoes, 1 cup (30 g) of baby spinach leaves, ⅓ cup (80 ml) of vegan mayo or hummus and ½ cup (70 g) of jarred roasted red peppers, drained and sliced.

PLANTAIN-CRUSTED TOFU BENNY

This brunch classic gets a decadent makeover with plantain-crusted tofu cutlets. A combination of nutritional yeast, savory spices, oil and water creates a thick paste that helps the plantain crumbs cling to the tofu, creating a crunchy exterior that is heavenly when paired with a buttery English muffin, ripe tomato and smoky potato hollandaise.

PREP TIME: 20 MINUTES • COOK TIME: 20 MINUTES • YIELD: 4 SERVINGS

PLANTAIN-CRUSTED TOFU
16 oz (453 g) extra-firm tofu
2 tbsp (17 g) nutritional yeast
½ tsp Indian black salt (kala namak)
½ tsp turmeric
½ tsp onion powder
¼ tsp sea salt
¼ tsp black pepper
2 tbsp (30 ml) olive oil
2 tbsp (30 ml) water
1 cup (40 g) plantain chips
Cooking spray

HOLLANDAISE
1 medium red potato, diced
¾ cup (120 g) raw cashews
⅓–½ cup (80–120 ml) water
4 tbsp (56 g) vegan butter, divided
2 cloves garlic
Scant 1 tbsp (6 g) smoked paprika
1½ tsp (7 ml) lemon juice
½ tsp Dijon mustard
1 tsp sea salt
¼ tsp turmeric
¼ tsp Indian black salt (kala namak)
¼ tsp black pepper

FOR SERVING
4 English muffins
2 large ripe tomatoes, sliced
Chives, finely chopped
½ cup (60 g) vegan bacon bits (store-bought or page 136)

Slice the tofu into ½-inch (12-mm)-thick slabs. Place the tofu on a clean kitchen towel. Cover with another towel, then set a heavy pan on top to press the tofu.

In a medium bowl, combine the yeast, black salt, turmeric, onion powder, sea salt and black pepper. Add the oil and water. Whisk to combine. Gently coat the tofu in the marinade. Set aside.

Make the sauce. Boil the potato and cashews until the potatoes are fork-tender, about 8 minutes.

Combine ⅓ cup (80 ml) of water, 2 tablespoons (28 g) of vegan butter, garlic, paprika, lemon juice, Dijon, sea salt, turmeric, black salt and black pepper in a high-speed blender. When the potatoes are soft, add them to the blender, along with the cashews. Blend on high until smooth and creamy, about 2 minutes. Taste and adjust the seasoning if needed. Add more paprika for smokiness or lemon juice for tang. Add a little more water to thin the sauce, if desired.

Process the plantain chips to a very coarse grain, then transfer them to a plate. Put a large frying pan over medium heat. Generously spray the pan with cooking oil. Coat each piece of tofu in plantain crumbs. Don't worry if they are not coated evenly. Add the tofu to the pan and fry until golden brown and crisp on the bottom, about 3 to 4 minutes. Spray the tofu with cooking oil, then carefully flip to cook the other side.

Meanwhile, toast and butter the English muffins. Put a slice of tomato on the toasted muffins, then top with tofu. Ladle the potato hollandaise over the tofu and top with chives and vegan bacon bits.

FRESH TIPS!

Add 2 tablespoons (30 ml) of olive or grapeseed oil to the pan before cooking the tofu to make it crispier.

Swap the plantain chips for crushed cornflakes if needed.

PESTO SCRAMBLED TOFU

This is one of my all-time favorite breakfasts and the absolute fastest, most satisfying way I've ever made tofu. The pesto creates a cheesy, savory crust on the tofu as it cooks, and because it's so thick and strongly flavored, there's no need to press the tofu. Use store-bought or premade pesto to make this in less than 10 minutes.

PREP TIME: 10 MINUTES • COOK TIME: 12 MINUTES • YIELD: 4 SERVINGS

PESTO

3 cups (60 g) fresh basil, stems torn off

½ cup (80 g) hemp seeds, sunflower seeds, cashews, walnuts or pine nuts

¼ cup (60 ml) olive oil

¼ cup (60 ml) water

2 tbsp (17 g) nutritional yeast

3 cloves garlic

1 tbsp (15 ml) lemon juice

¾ tsp sea salt

¼ tsp black pepper

SCRAMBLED TOFU

20 oz (567 g) firm tofu

Cooking spray

1 cup (149 g) cherry tomatoes, halved (see Fresh Tips! for substitutions)

Salt and pepper, to taste

FOR SERVING

4 thick slices sourdough or gluten-free bread

2 tbsp (28 g) vegan butter

Roasted potatoes (optional)

Make the pesto. Combine the basil, hemp seeds, olive oil, water, nutritional yeast, garlic, lemon juice, salt and pepper in a food processor and mix until well combined. Stop to scrape down the sides if needed.

Wrap the tofu in a clean kitchen towel and squeeze the water out as much as you can without crumbling it too much. Put a pan over medium-high heat. Spray generously with cooking oil.

Break the tofu into 1- to 2-inch (2.5- to 5-cm) pieces and put them in the pan. Cook until lightly browned on all sides, flipping very gently, about 5 minutes. Add the tomatoes and cook until they are slightly soft, another 2 minutes.

Stir half of the pesto into the tofu. Set aside a few tablespoons to top the finished dish if desired and save the rest for another recipe (Artichoke-Pesto Veggie Pizza [page 82] or Pesto Mac 'n' Cheese [page 50]).

Cook for another 2 to 3 minutes, letting the pesto form crunchy bits on the tofu. Be sure to flip very gently so the tofu doesn't crumble and become mushy. Taste and season with salt and pepper, if desired.

Toast and butter the bread. Ladle a generous scoop of tofu with tomatoes onto each serving plate. Serve with toast and roasted potatoes, if desired.

FRESH TIPS!

This recipe makes a soft, moist scramble, similar to soft scrambled eggs. For a crispier scramble, break the tofu into smaller pieces and add 2 to 3 minutes to the cook time.

Swap the cherry tomatoes for chopped kale and broccoli florets for a green-filled variation. (Cook until the broccoli is tender.)

BBQ CHICKEN PIZZA

With powerful umami flavors from tomatoes and soy, BBQ sauce is the ultimate sweet and savory ingredient. Paired with crispy vegan chicken, salty cheese, creamy dressing and sweet roasted onion, this pizza is truly an explosion of flavor. Dress it up with homemade Sliceable Farmhouse Cheddar (page 61) and cashew cream (page 93), or keep things casual with store-bought ingredients. Either way, this recipe is a winner!

PREP TIME: 15 MINUTES • COOK TIME: 12 MINUTES • YIELD: 4 SERVINGS

16 oz (453 g) prepared, raw pizza dough (store-bought, see Fresh Tips!)

½–⅔ cup (120–160 ml) tomato-based BBQ sauce

⅓ cup (50 g) thinly sliced red onion

1 cup (75 g) mushrooms, sliced or chopped

1 cup (140 g) chopped vegan chicken (store-bought or see Fresh Tips! for options)

1½ cups (180 g) shredded vegan Cheddar (store-bought or from page 61)

¼ tsp paprika

¼ tsp garlic powder (plus more, optional, for crust)

1 tbsp (14 g) vegan butter, melted (optional, for crust)

1 tbsp (2 g) cilantro, finely chopped

3 tbsp (45 ml) vegan ranch or cashew cream (optional, page 93)

Important—if you're using a store-bought frozen or precooked crust, follow package instructions. Otherwise, preheat the oven to 500°F (260°C). Stretch or roll out the dough to about ½-inch (12-mm) thickness and about 14 to 16 inches (36 to 41 cm) in diameter.

Spread the BBQ sauce in an even layer over the pizza dough. Smaller crusts will need ½ cup (120 ml). Larger crusts may need up to ⅔ cup (160 ml). Top with the onion, mushrooms, vegan chicken and vegan Cheddar. Sprinkle the paprika and garlic powder over the top. For extra flavor, brush the melted vegan butter over the edges of the crust (if using) and sprinkle with a teensy pinch of garlic powder.

Bake the pizza for about 10 to 12 minutes, or until the crust is golden brown. If using a frozen or precooked crust, follow the cook times on the package. Allow the pizza to cool for 1 to 2 minutes, then top with cilantro and a drizzle of ranch. Then slice and serve!

FRESH TIPS!

Pizza dough is easiest to work with at room temperature. If you have the time, set your dough out for 1 to 2 hours before you stretch it.

For homemade vegan chicken, you can use chopped cooked BBQ chicken (page 23) or a chopped crispy chickpea patty (page 12).

Get creative and add some tempeh bacon bits (page 136)!

ARTICHOKE-PESTO VEGGIE PIZZA

My new favorite way to eat vegetables: on a pizza with plenty of artichokes and pesto! The tanginess of the artichoke pairs beautifully with the umami cheesiness of the pesto. The flavors are further enhanced by savory mushrooms, sweet roasted onion, roasted red peppers and plenty of vegan mozzarella! This pizza tastes great with the pesto used in Pesto Scrambled Tofu (page 78), or you can use store-bought vegan pesto to save time.

PREP TIME: 15 MINUTES • COOK TIME: 12 MINUTES • YIELD: 4 SERVINGS

16 oz (453 g) prepared, raw pizza dough (store-bought, see Fresh Tips!)

½ cup (115 g) vegan pesto

¼ cup (40 g) thinly sliced red onion

1 cup (75 g) mushrooms, thinly sliced

½ cup (70 g) jarred roasted red peppers, thinly sliced

1 cup (168 g) marinated artichoke hearts, drained well and chopped

1½ cups (180 g) shredded vegan mozzarella (store-bought or page 58, see Fresh Tips!)

¼ tsp garlic powder (plus more, optional, for crust)

1 tbsp (14 g) vegan butter, melted (optional, for crust)

1 tbsp (2 g) fresh basil, finely chopped (optional)

2 tbsp (15 g) shredded vegan Parmesan (optional, page 57)

Important—If you're using a store-bought frozen or precooked crust, follow package instructions. Otherwise, preheat the oven to 500°F (260°C). Stretch or roll out the dough to ½-inch (12-mm) thickness and about 14 to 16 inches (36 to 41 cm) in diameter.

Spread the pesto over the dough. Don't be tempted to go too heavy on the sauce, since the veggies have so much moisture. We don't want a soggy pizza! Top with the onion, mushrooms, peppers, artichoke hearts and vegan mozzarella. Sprinkle the garlic powder over the top. For extra flavor, brush melted vegan butter (if using) over the edges of the crust and sprinkle with a teensy pinch of garlic powder.

Bake the pizza for about 10 to 12 minutes or until the crust is golden brown. If using a frozen or precooked crust, follow the package cook times. Top with basil and Parmesan after baking (if using). Let the pizza cool for 1 to 2 minutes before slicing and serving.

FRESH TIPS!

Pizza dough is easiest to work with at room temperature. If you have the time, set your dough out for 1 to 2 hours before you stretch it.

If using the Cashew Caprese Mozzarella (page 58), slice it into thin rounds and place on top of the pizza, margherita style. You can also freeze it until firm and then shred, if desired.

BROCCOLI CHEDDAR SOUP

What's typically a heavy, cream-laden soup gets a healthier makeover with a secret ingredient—blended white beans! The end result is every bit as thick, savory and satisfying, but so much more wholesome. The other wow factors of this soup? Smoked paprika and a dash of Dijon mustard! These enhance the cheesiness of the soup, allowing us to use less cheese and keep the soup on the lighter side. Use Sliceable Farmhouse Cheddar (page 61) or store-bought Cheddar to save time.

PREP TIME: 20 MINUTES • COOK TIME: 15 MINUTES • YIELD: 4 SERVINGS

3 cups (275 g) broccoli florets, 1 cup (90 g) stems (from 2 large crowns)

1 tbsp (14 g) vegan butter (see Fresh Tips!)

1 small yellow onion, diced

2 large cloves garlic, minced

¾ tsp sea salt, plus more to taste

½ tsp black pepper, plus more to taste

1 tsp smoked paprika

½ tsp Dijon mustard

⅛ tsp cayenne

1 large carrot, peeled and thinly diced

4 cups (960 ml) vegetarian chicken broth, divided (see Fresh Tips! for options)

1 (14-oz [400-g]) can white beans

1¼ cups (150 g) shredded vegan Cheddar, divided (store-bought or Sliceable Farmhouse Cheddar [page 61])

FOR SERVING

Crusty sourdough loaf

Parsley

Chop the broccoli into 1-inch (2.5-cm) pieces. Place a pan over medium-high heat. Melt the butter in the pan, then add the onion. Cook for 1 minute, then add the garlic and stir. Cook for 1 more minute, then add the salt, pepper, paprika, Dijon and cayenne.

Cook and stir for another minute, allowing the spices to develop the flavor. Add the broccoli, carrot and 3 cups (720 ml) of broth. Bring to a simmer and cook until tender, about 8 to 10 minutes, stirring occasionally. Meanwhile, drain and rinse the white beans, then add them to a blender with the remaining 1 cup (240 ml) of broth.

When the vegetables are tender, use a slotted spoon to add 2 cups (300 g) of broccoli and carrots to the blender. Blend with the beans and broth until smooth. Transfer the mixture back to the pot and bring to a simmer to thicken. Meanwhile, slice and toast the bread. Add 1 cup (120 g) of shredded vegan Cheddar. Mix well. Taste and add more salt and pepper, if desired.

Ladle into serving bowls. Garnish with the remaining ¼ cup (30 g) of Cheddar and parsley. Serve with crusty bread.

FRESH TIPS!

To make the oil-free version, omit the vegan butter. Add the onion to the pan with 2 tablespoons (30 ml) of additional broth. Continue the recipe as written, adding broth 1 tablespoon (15 ml) at a time to prevent sticking as needed. Use store-bought, whole-food, plant-based Cheddar shreds (check the label; you can find cashew-based cheeses in some health food stores) or use 1 cup (120 g) of Sliceable Farmhouse Cheddar (page 61).

Vegetarian chicken broth tastes more like chicken broth than vegetable broth, so I like to use it in most recipes that traditionally call for chicken broth. However, vegetable broth is a good swap if you don't have vegetarian chicken broth.

If using vegetarian chicken bouillon cubes mixed with water, keep in mind that the cubes are saltier than boxed vegetarian chicken broth. If you use this broth method, omit the listed salt amount and instead salt to taste.

NO-HUEVOS RANCHEROS

A lesson in vegan sauce making: salsa + cashews + spices = absolute heaven! In this recipe, the roasted bell peppers add a salsa-like rancheros vibe to the sauce, but the base is totally customizable. Experiment with chipotle peppers for chipotle aioli, green salsa for green enchilada sauce and so on!

PREP TIME: 20 MINUTES • COOK TIME: 20 MINUTES • YIELD: 4 SERVINGS

2 medium red bell peppers, chopped

¼ small white onion, sliced

BEANS

¼ small white onion, diced

3 tbsp (45 ml) vegetable broth or water

2 cloves garlic, minced

1 (14-oz [400-g]) can black beans, drained and rinsed

½ (4-oz [113-g]) can green chilis, drained

½ tsp cumin

½ tsp chili powder

Juice of ½ lime

⅛ tsp salt

RANCHERO SAUCE

¾ cup (120 g) raw cashews, soaked for 6+ hours or boiled for 10 minutes

1 cup (240 ml) tomato sauce or red salsa

2 cloves garlic

1 tsp cumin

1 tsp chili powder

Juice of ½ lime

¼ tsp cayenne

¼ tsp coconut sugar or maple syrup (optional, to balance flavors)

¼ tsp salt

½ tsp liquid smoke (optional)

RANCHEROS

1 batch Eggy Tofu Scramble (page 70)

1–2 tbsp (15–30 ml) grapeseed or avocado oil (see Fresh Tips!)

8 thick corn or flour tortillas

2 large ripe avocados, sliced

¼ cup (4 g) cilantro, chopped

Hot sauce

Preheat the oven to 450°F (232°C). Line a baking sheet with parchment paper. Spread the bell peppers and half of the sliced onion onto the sheet. Roast for about 10 minutes, until softened. Dice the remaining onion.

Meanwhile, prepare the beans. Put a small pan over medium-high heat. When it's hot, add the diced onion and broth. Cook for 1 minute, then add the garlic to the pan and cook for 30 seconds. Add the beans, green chilis, cumin, chili powder, lime juice and salt. Stir well. Cover and reduce the heat to low.

Make the sauce. Put the roasted bell peppers and onion in a high-speed blender with the cashews, tomato sauce, garlic, cumin, chili powder, lime juice, cayenne, sugar, salt and liquid smoke (if using). Blend on high until smooth and creamy, about 2 minutes.

Heat the tofu scramble. Put a large pan over medium high heat. Add 1 tablespoon (15 ml) of the oil. Working in batches, lightly fry the tortillas until crisp and golden brown, about 2 minutes on each side. Add more oil as needed. When the tortillas are crisp, transfer them directly onto serving plates, 2 per plate.

Top the tortillas with a large scoop of beans and tofu scramble. Pour the ranchero sauce over the top. Finish with avocado, cilantro and hot sauce.

FRESH TIPS!

To make the oil-free version, bake the tortillas on lined baking sheets for 3 to 5 minutes at 400°F (204°C) until crisp and slightly browned. All ovens and tortillas are different, so check them after 3 minutes and watch carefully.

If you don't have time to make tofu scramble, store-bought vegan egg works as an easy swap. I love JUST Egg brand.

MUSHROOM-ASPARAGUS BREAKFAST CREPES

Turn your kitchen into a cozy French café with these incredible savory breakfast crepes!
Tip #1—Use aquafaba as an egg replacer. It binds well while being nice and light, unlike chia or flax,
which would create a crunchy or dense texture. Tip #2—Use a thick milk like soy or oat. Thinner milks like
almond or rice will make a batter that's delicate and harder to flip in the pan.

PREP TIME: 35 MINUTES • COOK TIME: 30 MINUTES • YIELD: 4 SERVINGS

CREPES

2 cups (480 ml) soy or oat milk

2 cups (480 ml) aquafaba, from about 3 (14-oz [400-g]) cans of chickpeas

5 tbsp (75 ml) melted vegan butter, divided

1 tbsp (14 g) baking powder

½ tsp salt

2 cups (250 g) all-purpose flour (see Fresh Tip! for a gluten-free option)

FILLING

16 oz (453 g) asparagus spears, chopped into 2-inch (5-cm) pieces

16 oz (453 g) mushrooms, sliced

5–6 cloves garlic, minced

12 oz (340 g) spinach

Salt and pepper

1 cup (120 g) shredded vegan Cheddar (store-bought or page 61)

FOR SERVING

1 avocado, sliced

½ cup (120 ml) salsa

Combine the milk, aquafaba, 2 tablespoons (30 ml) of butter, baking powder and salt in a blender. Add the flour last. Blend for a few seconds until completely smooth. Let the batter rest for 30 minutes (this helps the crepes not to tear).

Preheat an 8- or 10-inch (20- or 25-cm) nonstick skillet over medium heat for 2 minutes. Grease with some of the remaining butter using a silicone brush or a butter-soaked paper towel. When the pan is hot, pour ⅓ cup (80 ml) of batter into the pan and swirl to coat the bottom of the pan. Lift the pan to swirl, and spread the batter along the edge first, then the middle. Try to create a very even layer.

Put the pan back over the heat. Cook until the edges begin to brown, about 40 to 60 seconds. When the crepe looks bubbly and no longer liquid, with browned edges, use a metal spatula to gently lift the crepe around the edges, then very carefully flip over. Cook for another 15 to 20 seconds.

Repeat until the batter is gone. Mix the batter each time before pouring another crepe into the pan. Stack the cooked crepes on a wire rack or plate. Brush a small amount of the remaining butter between each crepe to prevent sticking.

Prepare the filling. Put another pan over medium-high heat. Grease with the remaining butter. Add the asparagus and mushrooms. Cook for 4 to 5 minutes, then add the garlic and spinach. Season with salt and pepper. Stir and cook for 2 minutes, then stir in the cheese. Cook until the cheese has melted. Remove from the heat.

If you need to reheat the crepes before serving, cover them with a plate and microwave them for 30 seconds. Remove the plate quickly so the crepes don't get soggy from moisture. To build the crepes, place each one on a plate. Spoon the vegetable filling in the middle, then fold the sides over. Top with avocado and salsa, then serve.

FRESH TIP!

To make a gluten-free version, use an all-purpose, gluten-free flour blend that is gum-free and free of bean flours. The best ones will list sweet rice flour and tapioca flour (also called starch) as the main ingredients.

TOMATO JAM AND AVOCADO TARTINE

Level-up your basic avocado toast to a culinary delight with this easy tomato jam! It's sweet, tart, tangy and tastes complex, despite being super easy to make. A handful of vegan feta and microgreens is a lovely touch. Serve the dish on crostini for an elegant appetizer. Leftover jam also makes a nice complement to Mediterranean meals, especially the Marinated Farro and Arugula Salad Mezze Plate (page 113).

PREP TIME: 10 MINUTES • COOK TIME: 30 MINUTES • YIELD: 8 SERVINGS

1 shallot, diced

2 cloves garlic, minced

1 tbsp (15 ml) olive oil

4 cups (596 g) cherry or grape tomatoes, halved

⅓ cup (80 ml) apple cider vinegar

1⅓ tbsp (16 g) brown or coconut sugar

1 tsp ground ginger

¼ tsp salt

Dash of red pepper flakes

2 tbsp (4 g) basil, chopped

FOR SERVING

8 large, thick slices sourdough bread

4 ripe avocados (see Fresh Tips!)

½ cup (75 g) diced vegan feta (store-bought or page 62)

Salt and pepper

½ cup (8 g) microgreens

Put a saucepan over medium heat. Combine the shallot, garlic and oil. Stir and cook for 1 minute, until fragrant.

Add the tomatoes, vinegar, sugar, ginger, salt and red pepper flakes. Stir well and reduce the heat to medium-low. Simmer for 30 minutes or to your desired thickness. When the jam is thick, turn off the heat and stir in the basil.

Toast the bread. Slice the avocado. Layer your toast with tomato jam, sliced avocado and vegan feta. Top with salt, pepper and microgreens, then dig in!

FRESH TIPS!

The quality of the tomatoes matters a lot in this recipe! Try to use ripe, in-season tomatoes whenever possible.

Smashing the avocado into the toast first, then adding a sprinkle of salt, tomato jam, feta, microgreens and cracked pepper tastes better. Slicing the avocado and layering it on top looks prettier. Doing a combination of sliced and smashed is the best of both worlds!

FRESH

HOW TO BUILD THE PERFECT BOWL

PROTEIN
Round out your bowl with a big scoop of plant-based protein. My favorites include chickpeas, beans, peanut-baked tofu (page 102), smoky tempeh bacon (page 136) and BBQ soy curls (page 23).

GRAINS
A big scoop of grains adds texture and sustained energy. I love cooked quinoa, brown rice, black rice, sushi rice, rice noodles, soba noodles or marinated farro (page 113).

COLOR & CRUNCH
My favorite bowls include a rainbow of flavors and textures. I love adding bell peppers, roasted cauliflower, roasted sweet potato, watermelon radish, carrots, peas and sprouts.

GREENS
Start with a base of chopped lettuce, spinach, arugula, mixed greens or massaged kale (page 117).

SOMETHING TANGY
A pop of tang helps bring flavors to life! Use green or red onion, pickled ginger, pickled cabbage slaw (page 105) or a squeeze of citrus.

PLENTY OF SAUCE
A flavorful sauce can elevate a simple bowl to droolworthy status! My go-to's are BBQ sauce, cashew ranch (page 93), peanut sauce (page 114), miso dressing (page 105) or a even a large scoop of hummus.

HOW TO BALANCE BRIGHT AND DELICATE FLAVORS

Vegan food is known for being vibrant, colorful and fresh—a true celebration of plants! In this chapter, bright citrus notes and delicately balanced sauces allow fresh produce and herbs to take the lead. With a bright, luscious sauce full of lemon and fresh herbs, the Pan-Seared Tempeh with Lemon-Parmesan Cream (page 94) will have you licking your plate clean! Spring Linguine with King Oyster Scallops (page 97) brings a fresh, lip-smacking take on pesto.

When making these recipes, remember, one lemon might be significantly juicier or more tart than another lemon picked from the same tree. A box of rosemary can vary in strength and aroma from one you picked up the week before. Therefore, the key to balancing flavor is to taste often and make small adjustments as you go.

HOW TO LIGHTEN ANY DISH

One of my favorite aspects of plant-based cooking is feeling amazing after eating even a relatively large meal. Here are a few of the best easy ways to lighten any recipe!

SWAP IN CASHEW CREAM FOR MAYO

Instead of using mayo or oil, swap it 1:1 for cashew cream. To make cashew cream, blend 2 cups (320 g) of pre-soaked cashews with 1 cup (240 ml) of water until smooth and creamy. Season to taste with a pinch of salt and 1 teaspoon of lemon juice. This simple base works well in dressings, as sour cream or to make creamy sauces. Add ½ teaspoon of white pepper, ½ teaspoon of onion powder and 2 tablespoons (5 g) of minced chives to make vegan ranch.

LOW/NO OIL BAKING

Lighten up your baked goods by replacing some of the oil with an equal amount of applesauce, mashed sweet potato or mashed beets. Applesauce works well with lighter flavors. Sweet potato is great for spiced or chocolate recipes. Beets should be used in dark, rich chocolate recipes. You may need to increase the liquid in the recipe by a couple of tablespoons.

BROTH SAUTÉ METHOD

The first step in cooking with reduced or no oil is a quality nonstick pan. Instead of coating the pan in cooking oil, sauté the ingredients using vegetable broth or water, adding a couple of tablespoons (30 ml) at a time as needed to prevent sticking.

PAN-SEARED TEMPEH WITH LEMON-PARMESAN CREAM

This is a plant-based version of an insanely delicious-looking salmon recipe I found on Instagram. I chose tempeh to replace the salmon because both shine in dishes that have a slight sweetness to them like this one. Steaming the tempeh improves the flavor profile by reducing bitterness. It's not necessary when using bolder flavors, but in this case, it's nice because of the light flavors from the citrus, coconut and fresh herbs.

PREP TIME: 20 MINUTES • COOK TIME: 25 MINUTES • YIELD: 2 TO 3 SERVINGS

3 small zucchini

4 tsp (20 ml) olive oil, divided

¼ tsp salt, plus more to sprinkle

Pepper, to sprinkle

10 oz (283 g) tempeh

1¼ cups (300 ml) water

1 cup (170 g) whole-grain pearl couscous

1 tbsp + 1 tsp (18 g) vegan butter, divided

2 lemons

1 shallot, finely diced

2 large cloves garlic, minced

1 cup (240 ml) coconut milk

½ tsp red pepper flakes

½ cup (60 g) shredded vegan Parmesan (store-bought, see Fresh Tips!)

½ tsp brown sugar

2 tbsp (5 g) minced chives

2 tbsp (2 g) minced dill

FOR SERVING
½ cup (8 g) microgreens or arugula

Crusty baguette (optional)

Preheat the oven to 400°F (204°C). Line a baking sheet with parchment paper. Slice the zucchini into ¼-inch (6-mm) half moons. Place the zucchini on the baking sheet. Drizzle with 2 teaspoons (10 ml) of olive oil and sprinkle with salt and pepper. Mix to combine, then roast for 15 minutes, until tender. Stir halfway through cook time.

Slice the tempeh into ½-inch (12-mm)-thick triangles. Steam the tempeh in a basket over a small amount of water for 10 minutes. Bring the 1¼ cups (300 ml) of water to a boil in a small saucepan. Add the couscous, cover and reduce the heat to a simmer. Cook for 5 minutes, until the water is absorbed, then fluff with a fork.

Melt 1 tablespoon (14 g) of vegan butter in a large frying pan over medium-high heat. Add the steamed tempeh. Sprinkle with salt. Fry until golden brown, about 3 minutes on each side. Cut one lemon in half. Cut the other into slices.

Push the tempeh to the sides of the pan. Melt 1 teaspoon of vegan butter in the center. Add the shallot and garlic to the center. Place the lemon halves and slices cut side down next to the shallots. Press them down to get a nice sear. Cook the shallots for 1 minute, stirring occasionally. Remove the lemons from the pan when they're browned.

Add the milk, red pepper flakes, Parmesan, sugar and ¼ teaspoon of salt to the pan. Juice the halved lemon into the pan. Reserve the lemon slices to garnish the plate. Stir the sauce to combine. Flip the tempeh around to coat. Let the sauce reduce for a minute, then add the chives and dill.

Mix the zucchini into the couscous. Add the remaining 2 teaspoons (10 ml) of olive oil to the couscous and sprinkle with salt and pepper. Divide the couscous and tempeh among serving plates. Spoon the sauce over the tempeh and garnish with microgreens and grilled lemon slices. Serve immediately with a crusty baguette (if using).

FRESH TIP!

Store-bought vegan Parmesan works best in this recipe! It melts into the sauce and adds to the creaminess. Roasted Garlic Superfood Parmesan (page 57) won't have the same effect and isn't recommended for this sauce.

SPRING LINGUINE WITH KING OYSTER SCALLOPS

The stems from king oyster mushrooms make the most incredible plant-based scallops. These giant 'shrooms work well in place of seafood due to their natural umami-rich flavors and plump, succulent texture, especially when they are sliced into rounds, seared and cooked with a few key pantry ingredients to enhance the taste.

PREP TIME: 15 MINUTES • COOK TIME: 20 MINUTES • YIELD: 3 TO 4 SERVINGS

6 oz (170 g) brown rice linguine
Large pinch of sea salt

CHIVE-PARSLEY PESTO
⅓ cup (20 g) chives, packed
⅓ cup (20 g) flat-leaf parsley leaves, packed
⅓ cup (80 ml) olive oil
¼ cup (31 g) walnuts
2 cloves garlic
1 tbsp (15 ml) lemon juice
¼ tsp salt
Several cracks of black pepper
2 tbsp (30 ml) pasta water

ASPARAGUS
16 oz (453 g) asparagus spears, cut into 2-inch (5-cm) pieces
Pinch of salt and cracked pepper
2 tsp (10 ml) lemon juice
½ tsp garlic powder

MARINADE
1½ tbsp (22 ml) soy sauce or tamari
1 tbsp (15 ml) mirin
½ tsp lime juice
½ tsp garlic powder

KING OYSTER SCALLOPS
8 oz (227 g) king oyster mushrooms
1 tbsp (15 ml) mild cooking oil
2 tbsp (28 g) vegan butter

FOR SERVING
2 tbsp (15 g) shredded vegan Parmesan (optional)
½ lemon

Boil the pasta in salted water according to package instructions, then reserve 2 tablespoons (30 ml) of pasta water and drain.

Make the pesto. In a food processor, combine the chives, parsley, oil, walnuts, garlic, lemon juice, salt and black pepper. Process until smooth. Taste and adjust the lemon juice, garlic, salt and pepper if desired. Add the pasta water and blend until incorporated.

Lightly oil a pan and place it over medium heat. Add the asparagus. Season with a pinch of salt, cracked pepper, lemon juice and garlic powder. Cook for 2 to 3 minutes, until bright green and tender but with some crunch. Remove from the heat and set aside.

Make the marinade. In a shallow bowl, combine the soy sauce, mirin, lime juice and garlic powder. Stir well.

Make the "scallops." Slice the mushroom stems into 1-inch (2.5-cm) rounds, similar to scallops. Score the face of each piece with crisscrossed lines. Slice the caps into bite-size chunks.

Put a pan over high heat for 2 minutes and turn on the fan. This part can get smoky. Add the oil to the pan. Tilt the pan to evenly coat it. Using tongs, drop the mushrooms into the pan. Let the mushrooms cook undisturbed for 2 to 3 minutes, developing a nice sear. Drop the butter in little spoonfuls around the mushrooms, letting it run underneath them. This gives the scallops an unbelievably delicious, buttery crust!

Drizzle the marinade over the mushrooms, then flip. Sear the other sides until golden brown, about 3 minutes.

Combine the pasta, pesto, asparagus and Parmesan (if using). Divide between serving plates. Top each portion with scalloped mushrooms and a squeeze of lemon.

VIETNAMESE MANGO CHICKEN BOWLS

This vibrant, healthy bowl is fantastic for meal prep. It tastes amazing fresh, cold or at room temperature, and I think you're going to be shocked by how close this tastes to actual chicken. The lemongrass chicken can be easily adapted to any Asian recipe. You can try swapping the lemongrass for minced ginger. The possibilities are endless!

PREP TIME: 25 MINUTES • COOK TIME: 15 MINUTES • YIELD: 6 SERVINGS

2 (8-oz [227-g]) packages rice vermicelli

LEMONGRASS CHICKEN
8 oz (227 g) soy curls

4 cups (960 ml) hot water

¾ cup + 2 tbsp (210 ml) tamari, divided

4 stalks lemongrass (see Fresh Tips!)

1 large shallot, roughly chopped

6 cloves garlic, peeled

2 tbsp (25 g) coconut or brown sugar

2 tbsp (30 ml) water

½ tsp red pepper flakes

3 tbsp (45 ml) grapeseed or other mild oil, divided

FOR SERVING
2 heads green leaf or butter lettuce, rinsed and dried

2 large ripe mangos, sliced

6 Persian cucumbers, sliced

2 bell peppers, sliced

1½ cups (150 g) bean sprouts

½ cup (12 g) Thai or regular basil leaves

½ cup (46 g) mint leaves

⅔ cup (107 g) roasted peanuts or cashews

1½ cups (360 ml) hoisin sauce

Sriracha

Pour boiling water over the rice noodles. Let them soften for 7 to 8 minutes, then drain and rinse under cool water. Meanwhile, make the lemongrass chicken. In a bowl, combine the soy curls, water and ¾ cup (180 ml) of tamari. Stir well, then set aside to rehydrate for 10 minutes.

Peel the tough outer leaves from the lemongrass. Only use the bottom parts of the light, tender inner leaves. In a blender or processor, blend the shallot, garlic, lemongrass, sugar, 2 tablespoons (30 ml) of tamari, water, red pepper flakes and 2 tablespoons (30 ml) of oil.

Drain the soy curls, then wrap them in a clean kitchen towel and thoroughly squeeze out the liquid. Chop them into smaller pieces, if you prefer.

Heat 1 tablespoon (15 ml) of oil in a large pan over medium heat. When hot, add the soy curls. Cook for 2 to 3 minutes, until slightly browned, stirring occasionally. Pour the lemongrass mixture over the curls. Stir until well coated. Cook for 7 to 8 minutes, until slightly caramelized, then remove from the heat.

To serve, the first option is to leave the lettuce whole to use as lettuce wraps. Fill lettuce wraps with rice noodles, mango, cucumbers, bell peppers, bean sprouts, basil, mint and soy curls. Garnish with nuts of your choice. Serve with hoisin sauce and sriracha.

Or, you can serve this dish as noodle bowls. Shred the lettuce. Divide the noodles among serving bowls. Top each bowl with shredded lettuce, mango, cucumbers, bell peppers, bean sprouts, basil, mint, soy curls and nuts of your choice. Serve with hoisin sauce and sriracha.

FRESH TIPS!

Lemongrass can be found in the refrigerated produce section of most well-stocked grocery stores or Asian markets. You can also use 1 tablespoon (10 g) of lemongrass paste. If you can't find either, use 2 teaspoons (10 g) of minced ginger instead.

This bowl also tastes delicious with store-bought Thai ginger sauce or Peanut Stir-Fry Sauce (page 114).

MOROCCAN-ROASTED EGGPLANT WRAPS

Layers of tang from garlic, ginger, lemon and vinegar are enhanced with sweet paprika and fragrant cilantro to form chermoula—a traditional Moroccan sauce that just might be the most delicious sauce of all time! While typically served over fish or chicken, I chose smoky roasted eggplant to round out the tanginess of the sauce and really let the flavors shine. The result is seriously drool-worthy yet oh-so-simple to make!

PREP TIME: 25 MINUTES • COOK TIME: 20 MINUTES • YIELD: 4 SERVINGS

ROASTED EGGPLANT
2 medium eggplants
2 tbsp (30 ml) olive oil
½ tsp salt
¼ tsp pepper
¼ tsp garlic powder

CHERMOULA SAUCE
1½ cups (24 g) cilantro leaves, loosely packed
3–4 cloves garlic
2 tbsp (30 ml) water
1 tbsp (7 g) sweet paprika
Juice of 1 lemon
1 tbsp (15 ml) olive oil
Scant 1 tsp sea salt
¾ tsp quality balsamic vinegar
½ tsp agave
Scant ½ tsp ground ginger

FOR SERVING
4 pitas or 2 heads green leaf lettuce
⅔ cup (98 g) small tomatoes
2 small cucumbers
1 cup (250 g) hummus

Preheat the oven to 425°F (218°C). Line two baking sheets with parchment paper. Peel the eggplant so it is striped, leaving some of the peel on for texture. Chop the eggplants into 1-inch (2.5-cm) pieces. Put the chopped eggplant on the baking sheets. Try to leave space between the pieces if possible. Drizzle with oil. Season with salt, pepper and garlic powder. Toss gently, then roast for 18 to 20 minutes until the eggplant is tender but crisp.

Meanwhile, make the sauce. Pull the cilantro leaves and small stems from the thick stems. Discard the thick stems. Peel the garlic. Combine the cilantro, garlic, water, paprika, lemon juice, olive oil, salt, vinegar, agave and ginger in a mini blender or food processor. Blend until smooth, about 1 minute. Taste and adjust the spices if desired. Add more salt to enhance the flavors, more lemon juice to increase the tang or more agave if it tastes too bright.

Toast the pitas, if using, or rinse and dry the lettuce leaves. Halve the tomatoes. Slice the cucumbers.

Toss the roasted eggplant in the chermoula sauce. Spread a thick layer of hummus on each pita or lettuce leaf. Top each with a large scoop of eggplant. Garnish with the tomatoes and cucumber. Serve right away.

THAI CHOPPED SALAD WITH PEANUT-BAKED TOFU

Epic Tofu Tip: Coating your tofu in a seasoned nut butter mixture then baking it is a seriously delicious way to go.
Epic Salad Tip: A flavorful way to jazz up salads is to chop fresh herbs and mix them in with the greens.
For an even heartier meal, serve the salad over a bed of rice noodles and double the sauce.
You'll have leftover sauce, which I consider a bonus.

PREP TIME: 30 MINUTES • COOK TIME: 10 MINUTES • YIELD: 4 SERVINGS

10 oz (283 g) firm tofu

TANGY PEANUT DRESSING

½ cup (125 g) creamy peanut butter

3 tbsp (45 ml) soy sauce or tamari

3 tbsp (45 ml) rice vinegar

4 tsp (20 ml) lime juice

4 tsp (20 ml) maple syrup

3 cloves garlic

1½ tsp (3 g) minced ginger

2 tsp (4 g) red pepper flakes, plus more as needed

½ cup (120 ml) water

1½ tbsp (22 ml) sesame oil (optional)

2 tbsp (30 ml) soy sauce or tamari, divided

1½ tbsp (12 g) cornstarch or tapioca flour

FOR SERVING

16 oz (453 g) baby spinach leaves

6 oz (170 g) snap peas, trimmed

1 cup (110 g) shredded carrot

1 cup (70 g) shredded purple cabbage

3 stalks green onion, finely diced

1 large red or orange bell pepper, chopped

1 large ripe avocado, diced

⅓ cup (6 g) cilantro, chopped

½ cup (80 g) chopped peanuts or cashews (optional, for crunch)

Preheat the oven to 450°F (232°C). Line a baking sheet with parchment paper. Slice the tofu into 1-inch (2.5-cm)-thick slabs. Arrange the tofu in a single layer on a clean kitchen towel. Press the tofu by covering it with another towel and placing something very heavy—ideally a cast-iron pan—on top for 10 minutes.

Make the peanut dressing. Combine the peanut butter, soy sauce, vinegar, lime juice, syrup, garlic, ginger, red pepper flakes, water and sesame oil (if using) in a blender. Blend on high until smooth and creamy, about 1 minute. Taste and add more red pepper flakes to make it spicier, if desired.

Dice the tofu into 1-inch (2.5-cm) cubes. In a shallow bowl, drizzle the tofu with 1 tablespoon (15 ml) of soy sauce. Toss it gently with your hands, then drizzle the remaining tablespoon (15 ml) of soy sauce over it. Sprinkle the tofu with starch and gently toss until well coated. Add ¼ cup (60 ml) of peanut dressing to the tofu and gently toss to coat.

Place the tofu in a single layer on the baking sheet, with space in between each piece. Bake for 5 minutes, then carefully turn and bake for another 5 minutes, until browned and crisp.

Arrange the spinach, snap peas, carrot, cabbage, onion, bell pepper, avocado and cilantro. Top with tofu and nuts. Serve the peanut dressing on the side. Toss with the salad just before eating.

MISO RAINBOW VEGGIE BOWLS

The secrets to making the best bowls are plenty of crunch, a tangy element and an epic, creamy sauce. This flavorful bowl gets its tang from pickled cabbage, which can be made well in advance to speed things up. The miso dressing whips up in a jiff with pantry ingredients and vegan staples, making this the perfect easy dinner or meal-prepped lunch.

PREP TIME: 20 MINUTES • COOK TIME: 10 MINUTES
YIELD: 4 SERVINGS, PLUS LEFTOVER SAUCE AND PICKLED CABBAGE

PICKLED CABBAGE

1½ cloves garlic, minced

1 cup (240 ml) rice wine vinegar

1 cup (240 ml) water

⅓ cup (65 g) coconut sugar or agave

½ small head purple cabbage

1 tsp salt

¼ tsp red pepper flakes

MISO DRESSING

½ cup (137 g) white or yellow miso paste

2 tbsp (30 ml) soy sauce or tamari

2 tbsp (30 ml) rice wine vinegar

½–1 tsp sriracha, plus more for serving

1½ cloves garlic, minced

2 tbsp (30 ml) agave or coconut sugar

2 tsp (4 g) minced ginger

2 tbsp (30 ml) toasted sesame oil

½ cup (120 ml) water

FOR SERVING

4–6 cups (780 g–1.2 kg) cooked brown rice (use more for heartier bowls)

12 oz (340 g) baked or smoked tofu, diced into 1-inch (2.5-cm) pieces

2 cups (236 g) frozen edamame, thawed, then steamed

1 cup (136 g) frozen corn, thawed

3 carrots, peeled and shredded

½ watermelon radish, peeled and thinly sliced (see Fresh Tips!)

4 Persian cucumbers or 2 large cucumbers, sliced

2 avocados, sliced

Place the garlic in a medium saucepan, along with the vinegar, water and sugar. Place it over medium heat and bring it to a gentle boil. Shred the cabbage. Submerge the cabbage in the vinegar mixture. Mix in the salt and red pepper flakes, then transfer to a bowl. Place in the freezer to quick-pickle and cool for 15 minutes.

Make the dressing. In a small bowl, combine the miso paste, soy sauce, vinegar, sriracha, garlic, agave, ginger, sesame oil and water. Mix well. Add a bit more water to thin, if needed. Taste and adjust the seasoning, if desired. Add more soy sauce for saltiness, more agave for sweetness, more vinegar for sharpness, more sriracha for heat, more ginger for spice or more sesame oil to deepen the nutty flavor.

Warm the rice. Divide the rice among four bowls. Top with tofu, pickled cabbage, edamame, corn, carrots, watermelon radish, cucumber and avocado. Serve the miso dressing on the side.

FRESH TIPS!

Swap daikon or any other radish for watermelon radish as needed.

Use leftover pickled cabbage to jazz up bowls, burgers, burritos and more!

MARINATED TOFU POKE SOBA BOWLS

While oil is commonly found in marinade recipes, I don't use it when marinating tofu, because it can coat the tofu and prevent the marinade from sinking in. Also, since we're using sesame oil, which has a low smoke point, it's best to add it after cooking so the flavors don't burn off. Adding the sesame oil to the leftover marinade creates the perfect double-duty sauce without sacrificing flavor along the way.

PREP TIME: 35 MINUTES • COOK TIME: 15 MINUTES • YIELD: 4 SERVINGS

10 oz (283 g) firm tofu

MARINADE
½ cup (120 ml) rice vinegar
⅓ cup (80 ml) soy sauce
2½ tbsp (30 g) coconut sugar
2 heaping tbsp (12 g) minced ginger
4 cloves garlic, minced
1–2 tsp (2–4 g) chili flakes

NOODLES
6 oz (170 g) soba noodles
1 cup (150 g) snow peas
3 tbsp (45 ml) sesame oil, divided
Cooking spray

FOR SERVING
½ small watermelon radish, peeled and thinly sliced
4 small cucumbers, sliced
2 avocados, sliced
2 stalks green onion, diced
¼ cup (30 g) pickled ginger
1 jalapeño, thinly sliced (optional, for heat)
Black sesame seeds (optional, for garnish)

Drain the tofu and cut into 1-inch (2.5-cm)-thick slabs. Place in a single layer on a clean towel. Cover with another towel and put several heavy pots on top to press for 5 minutes.

Make the marinade. In a plastic container with a lid, combine the vinegar, soy sauce, coconut sugar, ginger, garlic and chili flakes. Mix well. Slice the tofu into 1-inch (2.5-cm) cubes. Add the tofu to the marinade, cover, then gently flip the container until the tofu is well coated. Set aside to marinate for at least 30 minutes, turning occasionally. The longer it marinates, the better it will taste.

Boil the noodles in salted water according to package instructions. Add the snow peas to the noodles for the last 2 minutes of cook time. Drain the noodles and peas, then rinse with cool water. Toss with 1 tablespoon (15 ml) of sesame oil to prevent sticking.

Put a pan over medium-high heat. Spray with cooking oil. Transfer the tofu to the hot pan with a slotted spoon. Cook for 3 to 5 minutes until brown, stirring every 30 seconds or so. While the tofu cooks, add 2 tablespoons (30 ml) of sesame oil to the remaining marinade. Drizzle half of the marinade over the tofu and reserve the rest.

Divide the noodles, snow peas and tofu among bowls. Top each with watermelon radish, cucumber, avocado, green onion, pickled ginger, jalapeño and sesame seeds (if using). Serve the remaining sauce on the side.

STRAWBERRY BISTRO SALAD

The ultimate bistro salad: mixed greens topped with ripe strawberries, vegan goat cheese, candied nuts and a basil mint dressing inspired by my travels through Morocco. The combination of sweet, tangy berries and basil and mint makes this salad taste like a warm spring day. For a more traditional bistro salad, swap the chickpeas for crisp vegan chicken.

PREP TIME: 20 MINUTES • COOK TIME: NONE • YIELD: 4 SERVINGS

DRESSING

1 small shallot, peeled and roughly chopped

¼ oz (7 g) fresh mint, stems removed

¼ oz (7 g) fresh basil, stems removed

¼ cup (60 ml) lemon juice

1–2 tsp (5–10 ml) agave

Dash of salt

¼ tsp cracked pepper

1–2 tbsp (15–30 ml) olive oil (optional)

2 (14-oz [400-g]) cans chickpeas

20 oz (567 g) mixed greens

2 cups (370 g) cooked quinoa, fluffed and chilled

¾ cup (125 g) strawberries, sliced

2 large cucumbers, very finely diced

1 cup (125 g) egg-free candied pecans or walnuts

¾ cup (112 g) vegan goat cheese or feta (optional, store-bought or page 65 or 62)

Make the dressing. In a blender, combine the shallot, mint, basil, lemon juice, agave, salt, pepper and olive oil (if using). Taste, then adjust the sweetness or seasoning, if desired.

Drain and rinse the chickpeas. (Save the liquid, a.k.a. aquafaba, for another recipe!) Divide the mixed greens and quinoa among serving bowls. Add the strawberries, cucumbers and chickpeas to each bowl. Top the salads with pecans and crumbled cheese, if using. Serve the dressing on the side.

FRESH TIP!

Find egg-free candied pecans or walnuts in the bulk bin of your local health food store.

CAULIFLOWER-AVOCADO CEVICHE

Cauliflower continues to blow my mind. It can be transformed into steak, rice, creamy sauces and now, ceviche! Steaming the cauliflower gives it a softened texture that works well in place of white fish. Plenty of lime juice delivers the tang you'd expect from a juicy bite of ceviche while the avocado adds a creaminess that just melts in your mouth. I love making this recipe on hot summer days, when entertaining guests, or just to munch on throughout the week.

PREP TIME: 20 MINUTES • COOK TIME: 5 MINUTES • YIELD: 6 SERVINGS

1 small head cauliflower

½ cup (120 ml) vegetable broth

¼ tsp garlic powder

Pinch of salt

½ cup (8 g) cilantro, packed

1 bell pepper

2 ripe avocados

2 Roma tomatoes

2 jalapeños

Juice of 4–5 limes

1–2 tbsp (15–30 ml) olive oil (optional)

⅓ cup (50 g) finely diced red onion

Salt and pepper, to taste

10 oz (283 g) tortilla chips

Trim the leaves from the cauliflower, then finely chop it into ¾-inch (19-mm) pieces. Place the cauliflower in a large pan over medium heat, along with the vegetable broth. Cover and steam until tender, about 4 to 5 minutes. Transfer to a medium bowl. Toss with the garlic powder and a pinch of salt. Place in the freezer to cool.

Tear the cilantro leaves and small stems from the larger stems. Discard the large stems, then mince the leaves. Deseed and finely chop the bell pepper. Pit and dice the avocados. Deseed and dice the tomatoes. Mince the jalapeños (keep some of the jalapeño seeds if you want a spicier ceviche; otherwise, discard).

Once the cauliflower is cool, add the lime juice, olive oil (if using), onion, cilantro, bell pepper, avocado, tomatoes, jalapeños and salt and pepper, to taste. Mix well. This dish can be eaten right away but tastes best when the flavors have had a chance to mingle in the fridge for at least 30 minutes. Serve with tortilla chips.

MARINATED FARRO AND ARUGULA SALAD MEZZE PLATE

This bright, tangy salad—described as a "dream dinner" by one of my beloved recipe testers—is not to be skipped! The chewiness of the farro and the crispness of the veggies deliver the perfect amount of texture and crunch. The herbs and citrus dressing highlight the flavors of the fresh produce while the hummus, pita and dolma make this a hearty, satisfying meal.

PREP TIME: 15 MINUTES • COOK TIME: 35 MINUTES • YIELD: 4 SERVINGS

1 cup (200 g) whole dried farro (see Fresh Tip!)

DRESSING
2 cloves garlic, smashed well and finely minced

¼ cup (60 ml) olive oil

2 tbsp (30 ml) red wine vinegar

2 tbsp (30 ml) lemon juice

½ tsp agave

2 tsp (2 g) dried oregano

½ tsp salt

10–15 cracks of black pepper

ARUGULA SALAD
¼ red onion

2 cups (298 g) small tomatoes

3 Persian cucumbers

3 cups (60 g) arugula

3 tbsp (17 g) minced mint, plus more for garnish

3 tbsp (11 g) minced parsley, plus more for garnish

FOR SERVING
4 pitas or flatbreads

1⅓ cups (330 g) hummus

1 (10-oz [283-g]) can dolmas (stuffed grape leaves)

¼ cup (34 g) pitted Kalamata olives

¼ cup (40 g) vegan feta (optional, page 62)

Boil the farro in water for 30 minutes, until soft but chewy. Meanwhile, make the dressing. Blend or whisk together the garlic, oil, vinegar, lemon juice, agave, oregano, salt and pepper. Taste and adjust the seasoning, if desired.

Prepare the vegetables. Finely dice the onion. Halve the tomatoes. Dice the cucumbers. Tear the arugula leaves apart a bit.

Drain the farro, then transfer to a large bowl. Pour the dressing over the farro. Mix the onion, tomatoes, cucumbers, mint, parsley and arugula into the farro. Place in the fridge for a few minutes to chill and marinate.

Heat a flat skillet. Lightly oil or butter the surface if desired. Cook the pitas for 1 to 2 minutes on each side, until warm and slightly crispy. Fill your serving plates with toasted pita, hummus, farro salad, dolmas and olives. Garnish with more herbs and feta, if desired.

FRESH TIP!

Save time by cooking the farro in a pressure cooker, or soak the farro in water overnight in the fridge. The next day, drain the water, replace with 3 cups (720 ml) of fresh water, then boil for 10 minutes instead of 30.

THE BEST DAMN PEANUT STIR-FRY

Whipping up the perfect peanut sauce is my favorite way to glow up end-of-the-week vegetables with a fabulously simple stir-fry. Start with soy sauce for saltiness, peanut butter for creaminess and water to thin. Then add rice vinegar, garlic and ginger for tang and brown sugar to balance the flavors. Sriracha adds heat while toasted sesame oil rounds things out with a silky mouthfeel and deep nutty flavor.

PREP TIME: 15 MINUTES • COOK TIME: 20 MINUTES • YIELD: 2 TO 3 SERVINGS

10 oz (283 g) firm tofu

2 tbsp (30 ml) soy sauce or tamari

½ tsp garlic powder

1 tbsp (8 g) cornstarch or potato starch

1 tbsp (15 ml) grapeseed or other mild oil, divided

1 cup (100 g) chopped cauliflower

4–5 cloves garlic

1 white onion, chopped

1 cup (134 g) chopped asparagus

1 bell pepper, chopped

PEANUT STIR-FRY SAUCE

4 tbsp (60 ml) soy sauce or tamari

3 tbsp (48 g) peanut butter

2 tbsp (30 ml) warm water

2 tbsp (30 ml) toasted sesame oil

1 tbsp (15 ml) rice vinegar

2 tbsp (25 g) brown sugar

2 cloves garlic, minced

4 tsp (12 g) minced ginger

2 tsp (5 g) cornstarch or potato starch

2 tsp (10 ml) sriracha, plus more for garnish

FOR SERVING

4 cups (780 g) cooked brown rice (see Fresh Tips!)

2 stalks green onion, diced

2 tbsp (18 g) peanuts, chopped

Wrap the tofu in a towel and gently squeeze out the water. Dice into 1-inch (2.5-cm) cubes. Put the cubes in a container with a lid. Drizzle the soy sauce over the tofu, then cover and shake until well coated. Add the garlic powder and starch, then cover and shake again.

Put a nonstick pan over medium-high heat. Pour in 2 teaspoons (10 ml) of oil. Cook the tofu until browned on all sides, about 3 to 4 minutes, turning occasionally. Remove the tofu when it's done and place the pan back over the heat.

Add the cauliflower to the pan, along with the remaining 1 teaspoon of oil. While it cooks, mince the garlic. Add the white onion to the pan. Stir and cook until the onion is soft, about 3 to 4 minutes .

Add the asparagus, bell pepper and garlic to the pan. Cook and stir until the vegetables are tender with a bit of crunch, about 5 to 7 more minutes.

Meanwhile, make the sauce. Whisk the soy sauce, peanut butter, water, sesame oil, vinegar, brown sugar, garlic, ginger, starch and sriracha together in a bowl.

When the veggies are tender with a bit of crunch, add the tofu back to the pan and turn off the heat. Add the sauce and mix well to combine. Serve over warm brown rice with green onion and chopped peanuts and a drizzle of sriracha, if desired.

FRESH TIPS!

Feel free to use other vegetables that might be hanging out in your fridge, like snow peas, broccoli or mushrooms.

Since brown rice can take up to 45 minutes to cook, I recommend prepping a batch ahead of time or using frozen brown rice for convenience.

CREAMY MASSAGED KALE AND QUINOA SALAD

It's fairly common knowledge that kale tastes better when massaged with fat, salt and citrus to break down the bitterness of the leaves. While most kale salads use oil for this, here, we swap in mashed avocado, which makes it extra creamy and satisfying, not to mention more nutritious! The creaminess is well balanced by apples for sweetness, fresh herbs for flavor and pickled cabbage for tang. This recipe calls for cooked and cooled quinoa, so it's best to make a batch the night before or at the beginning of the week to meal prep. Try it with Creamy Cashew Dressing (page 124) or use store-bought vegan ranch to save time.

PREP TIME: 30 MINUTES • COOK TIME: 5 MINUTES
YIELD: 6 SERVINGS, PLUS LEFTOVER DRESSING

SPICY PICKLED CABBAGE

1 cup (240 ml) apple cider vinegar

1 cup (240 ml) water

1 tbsp (15 g) cane or coconut sugar

2 tsp (12 g) salt

1 tsp chili flakes

1 clove garlic, finely minced

2 cups (140 g) finely shredded purple cabbage

10 oz (283 g) kale (about 2 bunches)

1 tsp salt, plus more as needed

1 large ripe avocado

2 tbsp (30 ml) lemon juice, plus more as needed

3 cups (555 g) cooked quinoa (cooled)

3 cups (447 g) cherry tomatoes, halved

2 apples, cored and diced

½ small red onion, thinly sliced

1 cup (136 g) pitted Kalamata olives

4 Persian cucumbers or 1 large cucumber, diced

1 (14-oz [400-g]) can chickpeas, drained and rinsed

½ oz (14 g) fresh dill or tarragon, finely chopped

1 cup (120 g) spicy pickled cabbage

FOR SERVING

1 cup (240 ml) vegan ranch or Creamy Cashew Dressing (page 124)

½ cup (75 g) vegan goat cheese or feta (optional, page 65 or page 62)

Fresh cracked pepper

1 large ripe avocado

1 lemon, sliced

Make the pickled cabbage. In a sauce pot, combine the vinegar, water, sugar, salt, chili flakes and garlic. Bring to a boil. Add the cabbage and boil for 2 minutes. If you're planning to use right away, transfer the cabbage and vinegar mixture to a bowl and place in the freezer to quick-pickle and cool. If making the cabbage ahead, transfer to a jar. Leave the lid off until it's cool, then cover and place in the fridge. The flavors will fully develop in 3 days.

Finely chop the kale. Put it in a large mixing bowl and sprinkle with salt. Massage the avocado and lemon juice into the kale with your hands, then set aside. This breaks down the leaves so they become softer and also reduces bitterness.

Add the quinoa, tomatoes, apples, onion, olives, cucumbers, chickpeas, dill and pickled cabbage to the kale. Pour the dressing over the salad. Mix well to combine. Taste and add a bit more salt and lemon juice if desired. Divide among serving bowls. Top with cheese (if using). Serve with a few cracks of black pepper, avocado slices and a wedge of lemon for squeezing.

SPICY

HOW TO BALANCE FLAVORS

To get the most out of spicy food—or any food, really—the flavors must be well balanced. Here's a cheat sheet for you to use the next time you're whipping up a meal without a recipe!

SALT

Salt enhances flavors. When flavors taste bland, increase salt using soy sauce, tamari or salty vegan cheese, like feta or Parmesan.

UMAMI/SAVORY

Umami ingredients add complexity and increase the overall savoriness in many dishes. Find it in tomato paste, nutritional yeast, kala namak and miso paste.

FAT

The richness of fats round out the fullness of flavors, making them more satisfying overall. Try using avocado, oils, nuts and seeds or coconut cream.

SOUR

Acidity livens the flavor palette. Achieve this with citrus or vinegar.

SWEET

Many savory recipes can benefit from ¼ teaspoon of coconut sugar, maple syrup, brown sugar or agave to balance flavors. Bold or spicy foods sometimes need a little more.

SPICY

A little bit of heat brings balance and complexity to a dish—think cayenne, chipotle and chili. Spicy dishes are well balanced by bold spices and sweetness.

THE JOY OF HEAT

This chapter is dedicated to everyone who is personally offended by bland food. There's just no reason for it! Food is meant to be savored and appreciated. If you're anything like me, a nice kick at the end of a delectable bite is one of the most enjoyable food experiences of all time. With that in mind, the recipes in this chapter are full of bold flavors and generous amounts of heat. Sink your teeth into a Cajun Caesar with Blackened Chickpeas (page 120) or dig into a hearty bowl of One-Pot Vegan Jambalaya (page 127). Lovers of milder foods can still enjoy the recipes in this chapter—simply reduce the heat by half or follow the modifications listed.

HOW TO COURSE CORRECT IN THE KITCHEN

TOO ACIDIC?

Often, a little sweetness will round out the flavors. Add fat for richness in the form of coconut cream, nut butter, cashew cream or oil. A long simmer will help too. In an emergency, add the teensiest pinch of baking soda to balance the acidity of a soup or chili.

TOO BLAND?

If all the flavors are there but need a little pop, add a bit of sea salt, soy sauce or tamari. For more tang, add citrus or vinegar. For bolder flavors, add more spices. To increase the umami flavors and overall complexity, add miso paste or nutritional yeast. Taste as you go and be careful not to overcorrect.

TOO SALTY?

This is trickier to correct. In a soup or stew, add a few chopped raw potatoes to absorb the salt. In most other dishes, try adding more grains or starch, more vegetables overall, or increasing the other flavor elements like fat, sweetness, spice and acidity.

CAJUN CAESAR WITH BLACKENED CHICKPEAS

If you're a Caesar salad fanatic like me, prepare to be blown away! Spicy Cajun dressing and blackened chickpeas elevate this meal from beloved classic to showstopper status. Crunchy romaine and creamy avocado perfectly balance the heat, while the chickpeas taste like crisp, chewy flavorbombs. I served this dish at a party, and it was devoured even faster than the truffle mac 'n' cheese. Bottom line—this salad is a must try!

PREP TIME: 20 MINUTES • COOK TIME: 25 MINUTES • YIELD: 4 SERVINGS

2 (14-oz [400-g]) cans chickpeas, drained and rinsed well

3 tbsp (45 ml) avocado or grapeseed oil

¼ cup (25 g) Cajun spice mix (store-bought or see Fresh Tips!)

CAJUN CAESAR DRESSING

1 cup (160 g) raw cashews, soaked for 6+ hours or boiled for 10 minutes, or hemp seeds

½ cup (120 ml) water

¼ cup (60 ml) olive oil

2 large cloves garlic

1 tbsp (9 g) nutritional yeast

2 tsp (10 ml) Dijon mustard

1 tsp vegan Worcestershire sauce

2 tsp (2 g) Cajun spice mix

1 tsp smoked paprika

1 tbsp (15 ml) lemon juice, plus more to taste

½ tsp salt, plus more to taste

CAESAR SALAD

3 hearts romaine, chopped or 2 (10-oz [283-g]) bags romaine

¼ cup (30 g) shredded vegan Parmesan (store-bought or page 57)

2 cups (80 g) croutons of choice (optional)

1 cup (149 g) small tomatoes, halved

2 ripe avocados, diced

Preheat the oven to 425°F (218°C). Oil two baking sheets. Dry the chickpeas very, very well. This is a crucial step in making them crunchy. If they aren't dry enough, they won't crisp up. I like to roll them around several times in a fluffy towel laid over the counter. Once you think they're dry enough, dry them even more!

In a large bowl, toss the chickpeas in the oil until evenly coated, then add the Cajun seasoning. Mix until well combined. Spread the chickpeas across the baking sheets. Make sure they are not touching much. Bake for 20 to 25 minutes, until very browned and very crunchy. Shake the pans halfway through cooking.

While the chickpeas roast, make the dressing. Combine the nuts, water, oil, garlic, yeast, mustard, Worcestershire sauce, Cajun spice mix, paprika, lemon juice and salt in a blender. Blend on high until smooth, about 1 to 2 minutes. Stop to scrape down the sides as needed. Taste, then add lemon juice or salt if needed. I like my Caesar dressing very thick, almost paste-like, but if you prefer a thinner dressing, add 2 to 3 extra tablespoons (30 to 45 ml) of water or olive oil. The salad is best served chilled, so pop the dressing in the fridge or freezer until ready to use.

Toss the romaine with the dressing, Parmesan and croutons (if using). Divide among serving bowls. Top with the blackened chickpeas, tomatoes and avocados. Serve immediately.

FRESH TIPS!

Not all Cajun spice mix contains salt. Check the label. If yours doesn't, add 1 teaspoon of sea salt when seasoning the chickpeas. Or, make a homemade blend using the mix below. There is a lot of seasoning on the chickpeas. It's normal for there to be a lot that blackens on the pan. If your chickpeas retained moisture after drying, they will require a longer cook time.

CAJUN SPICE MIX—Combine 2 teaspoons (4 g) of paprika, 2 teaspoons (2 g) of dried thyme, 2 teaspoons (4 g) of onion powder, 2 teaspoons (5 g) of garlic powder, 1 teaspoon of sea salt and ½ teaspoon of cayenne pepper.

PORTOBELLO-WALNUT CHORIZO HASH

This portobello-walnut chorizo deserves to be celebrated. The juiciness of the mushrooms, crunchiness of the walnuts and heat from the chipotle deliver all the spicy goodness of traditional chorizo and then some! Piled high on a bed of roasted potatoes, with a generous amount of vegan queso, this recipe makes the most epic vegan hash. Save any leftover chorizo to make breakfast burritos (page 70)!

PREP TIME: 10 MINUTES • COOK TIME: 30 MINUTES • YIELD: 6 SERVINGS

ROASTED POTATOES
3 lbs (1.4 kg) small gold potatoes

Cooking spray

1 tsp garlic powder

1 tsp smoked paprika

1 tsp sea salt

½ tsp black pepper

CHORIZO
1½ cups (190 g) walnuts

6 oz (170 g) portobello mushrooms

½ medium white onion

2 tbsp (30 ml) olive oil or vegetable broth (see Fresh Tips! for the oil-free version)

3 cloves garlic

2 tsp (2 g) oregano

2 tsp (4 g) cumin

2 tsp (8 g) coconut sugar

2 tsp (5 g) chipotle powder

½ tsp cayenne

¾ tsp sea salt

3 tbsp (42 g) tomato paste

¼ cup (60 ml) water

FOR SERVING
1 cup (240 ml) vegan queso (store-bought or page 54)

1 cup (240 ml) salsa

2 large ripe avocados, sliced or 1 cup (233 g) guacamole

Preheat the oven to 425°F (218°C). Line a baking sheet with parchment paper. Dice the potatoes. Scatter the potatoes across the baking sheet. Spray them with cooking oil, then sprinkle with garlic powder, paprika, salt and pepper. Toss them around a bit to evenly coat with spices. Bake for 15 minutes. Shake the pan a few times to turn the potatoes, then place them back in the oven for 10 more minutes until crispy and brown.

While the potatoes cook, make the chorizo. Place the walnuts in a food processor and pulse a few times. Roughly chop the mushrooms, then add them to the food processor. Pulse a few times until the walnuts and mushrooms are finely chopped. Be careful not to overprocess. Some texture should remain.

Place a pan over medium-high heat. While it heats, very finely chop the onion. Pour the oil in the pan, then scatter the onion in the pan. Let it cook while you mince the garlic. Add the garlic to the pan. Stir and cook for 30 seconds until fragrant, then add the walnut mixture. Stir to combine.

Add the oregano, cumin, sugar, chipotle powder, cayenne and sea salt. Stir well. Add the tomato paste and water. Stir well. Cook for 3 to 4 minutes, stirring often.

Warm the queso. Divide the potatoes among serving bowls. Top with a generous scoop of portobello-walnut chorizo, queso, salsa and avocado or guacamole. Serve immediately!

FRESH TIPS!

Use extra chorizo as a filling for tacos, burrito bowls, breakfast wraps or in a tofu scramble. The chorizo will keep in the fridge for 4 to 5 days.

To make the oil-free version, add the broth and chopped onion to a hot nonstick pan. Continue the recipe as written. Add broth 1 to 2 tablespoons (15 to 30 ml) at a time as needed to prevent sticking.

HOT HONEY CAULIFLOWER WINGS

While these sweet and spicy cauliflower wings don't taste exactly like chicken wings (and I'm SO okay with that!), they are crispy, bite-size, hearty and toothsome—just like the beloved bar snack! The sweetness of the agave balances the intense heat of the sriracha while the smokiness of the BBQ sauce adds dimension to the flavors. Dunk them in store-bought vegan ranch or make your own wholesome cashew version!

PREP TIME: 15 MINUTES • COOK TIME: 36 MINUTES • YIELD: 2 SERVINGS AS A MAIN, 4 SERVINGS AS A STARTER

CAULIFLOWER WINGS
1 small head cauliflower

3 tbsp (24 g) chickpea flour

3 tbsp (24 g) cornstarch

1 tsp garlic powder

½ tsp onion powder

½ tsp smoked paprika

½ tsp salt

½ tsp black pepper

¾ cup (180 ml) plain unsweetened dairy-free milk (anything but coconut)

1½ cups (75 g) panko breadcrumbs or gluten-free panko breadcrumbs

BBQ SAUCE
¼ cup (60 ml) agave

⅓ cup (80 ml) BBQ sauce

2 tsp–2 tbsp (10–30 ml) sriracha

FOR SERVING
Vegan ranch or Creamy Cashew Dressing (see Fresh Tips! for recipe)

Sliced carrots and celery (optional)

Preheat the oven to 400°F (204°C). Line two baking sheets with parchment paper. Trim the cauliflower into 2-inch (5-cm) wing-sized pieces. In a large bowl, combine the flour, cornstarch, garlic powder, onion powder, paprika, salt and pepper. Add the milk and whisk to combine. Pour the breadcrumbs into a shallow bowl.

Working a few at a time, dunk the florets into the batter, then coat in breadcrumbs. Arrange the florets in a single layer across two baking sheets, with plenty of space between the florets. If they're too close together, the cauliflower will end up steaming instead of crisping up.

Place the baking sheets side by side on a rack in the center of the oven. Bake for 30 minutes, gently turning halfway through. Meanwhile, combine the agave, BBQ sauce and sriracha. Start with 2 teaspoons (10 ml) of sriracha. Taste, then add more to increase heat.

When the wings are done, use a pastry brush to coat them in sauce. Tossing them in sauce will make them less crispy. Place the wings back in the oven for 5 to 6 minutes to crisp back up, then serve immediately with your favorite vegan dipping sauce and a side of sliced carrots and celery, if desired.

FRESH TIPS!

If you have an air fryer, use it for extra crispiness! Set the timer for 15 minutes, but check the wings after 10 minutes. Stop to turn halfway through.

If you're using a large head of cauliflower, double the amount of sauce and flour. This will increase prep time a bit. I use chickpea flour for added nutritional benefits, but feel free to swap it for all-purpose or gluten-free.

CREAMY CASHEW DRESSING—Combine 1 cup (160 g) of pre-soaked and drained cashews, 1 tablespoon (15 ml) of lemon juice, 1 cup (240 ml) of water, 2 cloves of garlic, 1 tablespoon (9 g) of nutritional yeast and ½ teaspoon of salt in a high-speed blender. Blend on high until smooth and creamy. Taste and adjust seasoning if desired. Use as a basic cashew cream or mix in 1 teaspoon of onion powder and 3 tablespoons (8 g) of minced chives to make a ranch-style dressing.

ONE-POT VEGAN JAMBALAYA

This spicy jambalaya is the perfect low-fuss recipe to feed a hungry crowd. Tender hearts of palm and succulent oyster mushrooms will make you wonder why you ever ate seafood in the first place! The addition of vegan sausage makes the most authentic jambalaya, but I also included a whole-food, plant-based version.

PREP TIME: 20 MINUTES • COOK TIME: 40 MINUTES • YIELD: 8 SERVINGS

---

3 bell peppers

2 ribs celery

1 white onion

16 oz (453 g) vegan sausage (see Fresh Tips! for a plant-based version)

6 oz (170 g) oyster mushrooms

1 tbsp (14 g) vegan butter (optional)

3 cloves garlic, minced

1 jalapeño

1 tbsp (8 g) chickpea or all-purpose flour

1 (14-oz [400-g]) can fire-roasted tomatoes, with liquid

3 cups (720 ml) vegetarian chicken stock

1½ cups (278 g) uncooked long-grain white rice

2 tbsp (16 g) Cajun seasoning

1 tbsp (3 g) dried thyme

1 tsp smoked paprika

¼ tsp cayenne pepper (optional)

1 bay leaf

1 (14-oz [400-g]) can hearts of palm, drained

2 cups (200 g) thinly sliced okra, fresh or frozen

Salt and pepper, to taste

¼ cup (15 g) parsley, loosely packed, chopped

2 stalks green onion, sliced

Dice the bell peppers, celery and onion. Thinly slice the sausage into rounds. Cut the mushrooms into 1- to 2-inch (2.5- to 5-cm) pieces. In a large pot over medium heat, cook the sausage and mushrooms for 4 to 5 minutes, stirring occasionally until the sausage is browned and mushrooms are tender.

Remove the sausage and mushrooms with a slotted spoon and set aside. Melt the butter in the pot (if using), then add the bell peppers, celery, onion and garlic. Let the mixture cook while you mince the jalapeño. Keep some of the seeds to increase the heat, if desired, otherwise discard the seeds. Add the jalapeño to the pot and cook for another 4 to 5 minutes, until the onions are softened.

Mix in the flour, then add the tomatoes, chicken stock, rice, Cajun seasoning, thyme, paprika, cayenne (if using) and bay leaf. Stir well to combine. Cook until the mixture begins to simmer, then reduce the heat to medium-low. Cover and simmer for another 25 to 30 minutes, until the rice is cooked through. Stir every 5 minutes so the rice doesn't burn.

Meanwhile, chop the hearts of palm into 1-inch (2.5-cm) pieces. When the jambalaya has about 5 minutes left to cook, uncover and stir in the sausage, mushrooms, hearts of palm and okra. Taste, then season with salt and pepper.

Ladle the jambalaya into serving bowls. Garnish with parsley and green onions. Serve right away or store in a closed container in the fridge for up to 3 days.

FRESH TIPS!

Some Cajun seasoning blends contain salt. Others have none. Be sure to check the label and adjust the salt accordingly.

I prefer the taste of brat-style Beyond Meat sausage for this recipe. If using a different type of sausage, add oil to the pan when cooking or use the broth sauté method (page 93).

WHOLE-FOOD PLANT-BASED VERSION—Omit the vegan sausage and double the hearts of palm and oyster mushrooms. Add 1 to 2 tablespoons (15–30 ml) of oil or broth to cook as needed. To make this without vegan butter or oil, use broth to deglaze the pan using the broth sauté method (page 93).

SHAKSHUKA AND GRITS

Shakshuka is a spicy North African stew typically served with poached eggs. It's a chili-like stew famous for its smoky spices, juicy peppers and low-key being the best brunch you've ever had. Here, I've swapped the eggs for polenta with a dash of Indian black salt, which creates an eggy vibe, both in flavor and presentation.

PREP TIME: 10 MINUTES • COOK TIME: 30 MINUTES
YIELD: 4 SERVINGS, PLUS LEFTOVER GRITS

GRITS
4 cups (960 ml) water

4 cups (960 ml) plain unsweetened soy milk

2 cups (320 g) coarse ground grits or polenta

1½ tsp (9 g) salt

½ tsp black pepper

2 tbsp (17 g) nutritional yeast

¼ tsp Indian black salt (also called kala namak, optional)

SHAKSHUKA
4 cups (596 g) ripe tomatoes

1 red bell pepper

2 tsp (10 ml) olive oil

½ onion, diced

2 cloves garlic

2 tsp (5 g) harissa powder

1 tsp cumin

1 tsp smoked paprika

2 tbsp (28 g) tomato paste

½ tsp coconut sugar

Salt and pepper, to taste

⅛–¼ tsp cayenne pepper, or more to taste (Careful, it's spicy!)

FOR SERVING
½ cup (75 g) vegan feta, chopped (optional, page 62)

2 tbsp (8 g) flat-leaf parsley, chopped (optional)

Combine the water and milk in a medium sauce pot. Bring to a boil. Add the grits, salt and pepper. Reduce the heat to medium-low and simmer for 20 minutes, until the grits are thick and creamy. Stir well, every minute or so, to prevent lumps and sticking. Once thickened, stir in the yeast and Indian black salt (if using).

While the grits cook, make the shakshuka. Dice the tomatoes. Deseed and chop the bell pepper into ½-inch (12-mm) pieces.

Put a pan over medium heat. Pour in the olive oil. While it heats, finely dice the onion. Add it to the pan. Cook for 1 to 2 minutes, until translucent. Meanwhile, mince the garlic. Add it to the pan. Cook and stir for 30 seconds, until fragrant.

Add the bell peppers and stir. Cook for 3 to 5 minutes or so, stirring occasionally, until softened. Add the harissa, cumin and paprika. Cook and stir for another 2 minutes.

Add the tomatoes and tomato paste to the pan. Stir until evenly mixed. Sprinkle with sugar and simmer for 5 to 7 minutes, until the mixture starts to reduce.

Taste the stew and add or adjust the salt, sugar, spices and cayenne, if desired. Reduce the heat to medium-low and simmer for 10 to 15 minutes, until thickened.

Ladle the shakshuka into serving bowls. Top each bowl with several dollops of grits, vegan feta and parsley.

FRESH TIPS!

Use the leftover grits along with vegan breakfast sausage (page 33) and roasted potatoes and tofu scramble (page 70) to make Southern breakfast bowls!

If you prefer not to have leftover grits, cut the grits recipe in half.

Save time by using store-bought vegan feta.

JAPANESE MUSHROOM CURRY

Fresh, plump udon noodles are the secret to this luscious Japanese curry, which is slightly sweeter and more savory than Thai or Indian curry. Unlike curries made with coconut milk, this Japanese curry uses mushroom broth for a deep umami flavor. Grated apple and a splash of rice wine enhance the dish with a touch of sweetness that's not to be missed!

PREP TIME: 5 MINUTES • COOK TIME: 50 MINUTES • YIELD: 4 SERVINGS

1 small white onion

6 fresh shiitake mushrooms

8 oz (227 g) crimini mushrooms

1 tbsp (14 g) vegan butter

6 oz (170 g) vegan beef (optional)

2 medium carrots

1 medium Yukon Gold potato

2 tbsp (30 ml) mirin rice wine or sake

4 cups (960 ml) mushroom broth

1 tbsp (15 ml) low-sodium soy sauce or tamari

1 tsp chili flakes, plus more to taste

½ Fuji apple

1 (3-oz [85-g]) box Japanese curry roux

16 oz (453 g) fresh or frozen udon noodles

Pinch of sea salt

2 scallions, sliced

Black sesame seeds (optional, for garnish)

Thinly slice the onion with the grain into 1-inch (2.5-cm)-thick pieces and the shiitake mushrooms into ¼-inch (6-mm)-thick slices. Cut the crimini mushrooms in half.

In a medium pot, melt the butter over medium-high heat. Add the shiitakes, criminis, onion and vegan beef (if using). Cook until the mushrooms and onions begin to soften, about 4 to 5 minutes.

Meanwhile, peel the carrots. Chop the carrots and potato into 1-inch (2.5-cm) pieces.

Add the mirin to the pot. Stir and cook for about 30 seconds, then add the carrots, potato, broth, soy sauce and chili flakes. Bring to a boil, then reduce the heat to between medium and medium-low. Meanwhile, peel and grate the apple, then add it to the pot.

Simmer until the vegetables are very tender, stirring occasionally, 25 to 30 minutes. While they cook, place a pot of water over high heat for the udon noodles.

Stir the curry roux into the vegetables. Mix very well until it dissolves. Cook until the stew is thick, about 6 to 8 more minutes. Meanwhile, cook the udon noodles. For frozen udon, boil for about 1 minute. For fresh udon, boil for 3 minutes. Drain the noodles but do not rinse, or they'll become sticky.

Taste the curry and season with a pinch of salt or more chili flakes, if desired. Divide the noodles among four large soup bowls. Top each with a generous ladle of curry and a handful of scallions, and sprinkle with black sesame seeds, if desired. Serve immediately.

FRESH TIPS!

Find fresh or frozen udon noodles at your local Asian market, where you'll also find Japanese curry roux (also called "blocks"). Look for S&B Golden or Torokeru Curry, or House Foods Java Curry.

If you can't find fresh or frozen udon, opt to serve the curry over 6 cups (1.2 kg) of steamed white rice instead of using dried udon, which can be rather flat and lifeless.

SPICY GARLIC RAMEN

How to make epic vegan ramen: blend creamy nuts with deep umami flavors and plenty of garlic.
Fry up some tofu and your favorite veggies, throw in some noodles, and you're done! It's a quick,
easy dinner that's always a crowd-pleaser.

PREP TIME: 15 MINUTES • COOK TIME: 25 MINUTES • YIELD: 4 SERVINGS

½ cup (65 g) brazil nuts, roughly chopped

1 large shallot, chopped

7–8 cloves garlic, chopped

2 tsp (4 g) minced ginger

1½ tsp (7 g) chili flakes (or to taste)

2 tbsp (30 ml) grapeseed oil, divided

14 oz (400 g) firm tofu

4 dried shiitake mushrooms

6 cups (1.4 L) mushroom broth (if unavailable use vegetable broth and increase the dried shiitakes to 6)

5 tbsp (75 ml) soy sauce or tamari, divided

1 tsp garlic powder

1 tbsp (8 g) cornstarch

2 cups (185 g) broccoli florets, chopped

6 oz (170 g) crimini or fresh shiitake mushrooms, sliced

3 (9-oz [255-g]) bundles of ramen noodles

⅓ cup (91 g) miso paste

2 tbsp (30 ml) sesame oil

FOR SERVING
2 stalks green onions

1 tbsp (15 ml) chili oil (optional)

In a medium saucepan, over medium-low heat, cook the brazil nuts, shallot, garlic, ginger, chili flakes and 1 tablespoon (15 ml) of grapeseed oil for 8 to 10 minutes, until the shallots are soft and browned.

Meanwhile, drain the tofu. Cut it into thick slabs. Arrange the tofu on a kitchen towel in a single layer. Cover with another towel and place a cast-iron pan on top to press for 5 minutes.

Rinse the dried shiitake mushrooms, then chop them and put them in the pan, followed by the broth. Increase the heat to medium-high and simmer until the shiitakes are soft, about 5 to 7 minutes.

Meanwhile, slice the tofu into cubes. Toss it with 2 tablespoons (30 ml) of soy sauce and garlic powder, then gently toss with cornstarch. Place an extra-large frying pan over medium-high heat. If you don't have an extra-large pan, use two medium pans to cook the tofu and vegetables separately.

Spread 1 tablespoon (15 ml) of oil in the pan, then add the tofu in a single layer. Let it cook, undisturbed, for 2 to 3 minutes, until the bottom is browned and crisp. Flip the tofu and push it to the side of the pan. Add the broccoli and crimini mushrooms to the other side, in their own piles. Drizzle the entire pan with 1 tablespoon (15 ml) of soy sauce. Stir the tofu, broccoli and mushrooms separately, until each pile is well coated. Cook until the vegetables are tender, 8 to 10 minutes, stirring often.

In another pot, boil the ramen noodles according to the package instructions, then drain and rinse.

Transfer the broth mixture to a blender. Add the miso paste, sesame oil and 2 tablespoons (30 ml) of soy sauce. Start the blender on low and slowly increase speed to avoid spilling. Blend until completely smooth. The liquid will be very hot. Be sure to vent the lid to let steam escape.

Thinly slice the green onions. Use the white and light green parts.

Divide the noodles among four large serving bowls. Top with tofu, mushrooms and broccoli. Fill the bowls with broth. Garnish with green onion and chili oil (if using).

TANDOORI-ROASTED WHOLE CAULIFLOWER WITH MINT CHUTNEY

The secret to roasting a head of cauliflower is to place a pan of water at the bottom of the oven so the inside of the cauliflower steams as the outer layer roasts. This roasting method can easily be customized with BBQ sauce, pesto or your favorite sauce to make a wide variety of meals! For a quick weeknight version, break the cauliflower into florets, toss in the marinade and roast until tender with some crunch, about 20 minutes.

PREP TIME: 15 MINUTES • COOK TIME: 35 MINUTES • YIELD: 4 SERVINGS

TANDOORI CAULIFLOWER
⅔ cup (100 g) tandoori spice blend (store-bought or see Fresh Tips! for recipe)

2-inch (5-cm) knob fresh ginger, peeled and chopped

4 cloves garlic, chopped

½ cup (120 ml) olive oil

½ cup (120 ml) plain coconut yogurt

Juice of 2 limes

4 tsp (24 g) salt

4 tsp (20 ml) agave nectar

2 small heads cauliflower (about 2–2½ lbs [900 g–1.1 kg] each)

MINT CHUTNEY SAUCE
1 cup (92 g) mint leaves

2 cloves garlic

½ cup (8 g) cilantro leaves

2 small Indian or Serrano green chilis, seeds and stem removed

Juice of ½ lemon

2 tsp (10 ml) agave nectar

½ tsp cumin

¼ tsp sea salt

FOR SERVING
6 cups (1.1 kg) cooked quinoa

¼ cup (30 g) sliced almonds (optional, for crunch)

Chopped cilantro

½ cup (120 ml) plain coconut yogurt

Preheat the oven to 400°F (204°C). In a hot, dry pan, toast the tandoori spice over medium-low heat for 1 to 2 minutes until fragrant, stirring every so often. Then combine the tandoori spice, ginger, garlic, olive oil, yogurt, lime juice, salt and agave in a blender. Blend until smooth.

Rinse and pat the cauliflower dry. Carefully trim away the stalks and green leaves, leaving the heads intact. Make several cuts to the stems and insides of the cauliflower heads. Place the heads cut side up in a baking pan. Pour most of the sauce over the bases. The sauce is thick, so use a pastry brush to push it into all the crevices. Flip the cauliflower heads cut side down. Brush the remaining sauce over them, including what spilled on the pan.

Put a pan of water on the bottom of the oven. Bake for 35 minutes, until easily pierced with a fork. Increase the heat to 500°F (260°C) for the last 5 minutes to brown the exterior.

Make the mint chutney. Combine the mint, garlic, cilantro, chilis, lemon juice, agave, cumin and salt in a blender and blend until smooth.

Serve the roasted cauliflower heads on a platter of quinoa, dressed with sliced almonds (if using) and chopped cilantro. Drizzle the mint chutney on top and serve with coconut yogurt on the side.

FRESH TIP!

The size of cauliflower matters a lot in this recipe. Don't use one large head instead of two small heads. A medium head should be okay but might require extra cook time.

TANDOORI SPICE BLEND—Combine 1 tablespoon (7 g) of paprika, 1 tablespoon (6 g) of garam marsala, 1 tablespoon (6 g) of cumin, 1 teaspoon of coriander, 1 teaspoon of turmeric and ½ teaspoon of cayenne.

BUFFALO TEMPEH BLTs

This sandwich is the perfect way to satisfy a buffalo craving without the heaviness of a butter-based sauce or fried food. White vinegar replaces the lemon juice in traditional hummus, hot sauce brings the heat and smoked paprika adds smokiness. Spicy buffalo hummus is the perfect spread to complement the smoky sweet tempeh bacon—my favorite of all plant-based bacon alternatives. Tempeh is naturally chewy, nutty and pairs well with sweet flavors. With a simple marinade of soy sauce, coconut sugar and liquid smoke, this tempeh bacon gets dark, sticky and very bacon-esque. Save leftover tempeh bacon or double the batch to make Baked Tofu Club Sandwiches (page 74).

PREP TIME: 10 MINUTES • COOK TIME: 10 MINUTES • YIELD: 4 SERVINGS

TEMPEH BACON
16 oz (453 g) tempeh

6 cloves garlic

6 tbsp (90 ml) soy sauce or tamari

4 tbsp (50 g) coconut sugar

1 tsp liquid smoke

2 tsp (10 ml) red hot sauce

BUFFALO HUMMUS
1 (14-oz [400-g]) can chickpeas, drained

¼ cup (60 ml) tahini

3 cloves garlic

3–4 tbsp (45–60 ml) red hot sauce

1 tbsp (15 ml) vegan Worcestershire

2 tbsp (30 ml) white vinegar

2 tbsp (30 ml) olive oil

2 tbsp (30 ml) water

1 tsp smoked paprika

Cooking spray

FOR SERVING
8–12 slices multigrain or gluten-free bread

2 large tomatoes, sliced

8 lettuce leaves

Slice the tempeh into ½-inch (12-mm)-thick strips. Peel and press the garlic. If you don't have a press, finely mince the garlic and use the back of your knife to smash and press it into a paste. In a medium container with a lid, combine the garlic paste with the soy sauce, sugar, liquid smoke and hot sauce. Add the tempeh to the marinade and put the lid on. Shake well until the tempeh is thoroughly coated.

Make the hummus. In a food processor, combine the chickpeas, tahini, garlic, hot sauce, vegan Worcestershire, vinegar, oil, water and paprika. Process until smooth and creamy. Stop to scrape down the sides as needed.

Put a griddle pan over medium heat. Spray with oil. Use a slotted spoon to transfer the tempeh to the hot pan. Cook until brown and crispy on one side, about 3 to 4 minutes. Drizzle the remaining marinade on the tempeh, then flip it over and cook until dark and sticky, another 3 to 4 minutes. Meanwhile, lightly toast the bread.

Build your sandwiches with a thick layer of buffalo hummus, tomato, lettuce and several strips of tempeh bacon. To make it a club-style sandwich, use 3 slices of bread per sandwich.

FRESH TIPS!

Use 3 tablespoons (45 ml) of hot sauce in your hummus for mild buffalo flavor. Increase for more heat.

To save time, use store-bought hummus. Stir 1 to 2 tablespoons (15 to 30 ml) of hot sauce, 2 teaspoons (10 ml) of Worcestershire sauce and 1 teaspoon of smoked paprika into 1 cup (250 g) of store-bought hummus. Omit the garlic, vinegar, tahini and oil. Taste and adjust spices if desired.

SPICY HARISSA FALAFEL

For the days when basic falafel just won't do! Harissa spice brings the heat with a bold, smoky flavor that's perfectly balanced by the slight sweetness of shredded carrots and a touch of maple syrup. These spicy patties are perfect for an easy lunch or dinner. See Fresh Tips! for a baked version.

PREP TIME: 30 MINUTES • COOK TIME: 10 MINUTES • YIELD: 4 SERVINGS

1 tbsp (7 g) ground flaxseed

2½ tbsp (37 ml) water

1 cup (90 g) oats

1 (14-oz [400-g]) can chickpeas, drained and rinsed

1 cup (110 g) grated carrot

2–3 cloves garlic, roughly chopped

1 large shallot, roughly chopped

½ cup (30 g) parsley, chopped

1 tbsp (15 ml) grapeseed or olive oil

1½ tsp (9 g) salt

1 tbsp (6 g) cumin

1½ tbsp (12 g) harissa spice blend or 3 tbsp (48 g) harissa paste (see Fresh Tips!)

¼ tsp cayenne

¼ tsp maple syrup

¼ cup (40 g) hemp seeds (see Fresh Tips!)

½ cup (25 g) panko or gluten-free panko breadcrumbs

½ cup (120 ml) grapeseed oil, for frying (see Fresh Tips! for baking method)

FOR SERVING

4 pitas

2–3 tbsp (30–45 ml) sriracha

1 cup (250 g) hummus

4 small cucumbers

Fresh veggies of choice

Whisk together the flaxseed and water in a large bowl. Tilt the bowl while you stir. Mix well and set aside.

Process the oats in a food processor to a flour, about 10 to 15 seconds. Add the chickpeas, carrot, garlic, shallot, parsley, oil, salt, cumin, harissa, cayenne and maple syrup to the food processor. Process to a chunky paste. Stop to scrape down the sides as needed.

Transfer the mixture to the flaxseed bowl and combine. Stir in the hemp seeds. Chill for 15 minutes in the freezer. Once chilled, form into six even balls, then flatten them into ½-inch (12-mm)-thick patties. Coat the patties with breadcrumbs. Use your hands to press the breadcrumbs into the patties.

Put a large pan over medium to medium-high heat. Add ¾ inch (19 mm) of oil and heat for 2 minutes. Drop a sprinkle of salt into the oil. When it sizzles, the oil is ready. Working in two batches, pan-fry each patty until deep brown and crunchy, about 3½ to 4 minutes on each side. Place on paper towels to drain.

Warm the pita. Stir the sriracha into the hummus. Slice the cucumbers. Serve the falafel with warm pita, hummus, cucumbers and veggies.

FRESH TIPS!

The fine texture of the hemp seeds helps the patties hold their shape. Omit the hemp seeds if you don't have any on hand. Do not attempt to swap a different nut or seed in for the hemp seeds, or the patties may fall apart.

If using harissa paste, add 1 tablespoon (8 g) of flour (any kind) to account for the extra moisture.

REDUCED OIL BAKING METHOD—Preheat the oven to 425°F (218°C). Line a baking sheet with parchment paper. When the dough is chilled, portion into balls with ⅓ cup (80 g) of dough each. Flatten them to ½-inch (12-mm) thickness. Arrange them in an even layer on the baking sheet, not touching. Bake for 15 minutes, then flip and bake for another 12 to 15 minutes. While the baking method is obviously healthier, the fried method will deliver a richer, more authentic falafel taste.

BAKED CHIPOTLE BLACK BEAN TAQUITOS

Lovers of healthy snack foods will be obsessed with this simple recipe. Adding cumin, chili powder, lime juice and salt to a humble can of refried beans creates a boldly seasoned taquito filling with plenty of heat and acidity. A variety of dips and toppings elevate this recipe from simple snack to light but satisfying dinner. Use store-bought Cheddar to save time or try with Red Pepper Cheese (page 49) or Sliceable Farmhouse Cheddar (page 61).

PREP TIME: 10 MINUTES • COOK TIME: 20 MINUTES • YIELD: 2 SERVINGS AS A MAIN, 4 SERVINGS AS A STARTER

1 cup (240 g) refried black or pinto beans

1 tsp lime juice

1 tsp cumin

1 tsp chili or chipotle powder

Salt, to taste

1 cup (120 g) shredded vegan Cheddar (store-bought or page 49 or page 61)

8 large corn tortillas

FOR SERVING

Vegan sour cream or cashew cream (page 93)

Sliced avocado or guacamole

Pico de gallo or salsa

Chopped cilantro (optional)

Preheat the oven to 400°F (204°C). Line a baking sheet with parchment paper. In a bowl, combine the refried beans, lime juice, cumin, chili powder and salt. Stir well. Taste and add more salt or spices, if desired. Then fold the cheese into the beans.

Wrap the tortillas in layers of wet paper towels. Microwave for 2 minutes. You want them to be moist and soft, so they don't crack when rolling or baking. Spread a thick tube-shaped layer of the bean and cheese mixture, about 3 tablespoons (50 g), in the middle of a tortilla. Wrap it up tightly.

Place the taquitos seam side down on the baking sheet. Repeat until all the bean and cheese mixture has been used. Bake for 16 to 18 minutes, until crispy. Flip halfway through.

Allow the taquitos to cool slightly before serving. Or just shove them in your mouth and burn your tongue like I did! Serve with vegan sour cream, guacamole and pico de gallo and sprinkled with chopped cilantro, if desired.

FRESH TIPS!

For a crispier, more traditional taquito, fry the taquitos in a ½ inch (12 mm) of hot cooking oil until crisp on all sides, about 5 minutes.

If you don't have a microwave, steam the tortillas in a steamer or tortilla basket placed over a small amount of boiling water until soft and pliable.

CURRIED ROOT VEGETABLE AND LENTIL SOUP

A peek behind the curtain of spicy soup creation: I chose apples, carrot and sweet potato to create a natural sweetness that complements the heat of the curry, the creaminess of the coconut milk and the tanginess of the lime juice. Red or yellow lentils are a must for this recipe for their speedy cook time!

PREP TIME: 20 MINUTES • COOK TIME: 35 MINUTES • YIELD: 6 SERVINGS

ROASTED VEGETABLES

3 medium carrots, peeled and diced

1 medium white or yellow onion, chopped

1 apple, cored and diced

1 medium sweet potato, peeled and diced

1 tbsp (15 ml) melted coconut or grapeseed oil (optional)

Salt and pepper

SOUP

1 tbsp (6 g) curry powder

¼ tsp cayenne

2 tsp (4 g) cumin

1 tbsp (15 ml) coconut or grapeseed oil

2–3 cloves garlic, minced

1-inch (2.5-cm) knob ginger, peeled and minced

1 (14-oz [412-ml]) can light coconut milk, divided

2 cups (384 g) red or yellow lentils (see Fresh Tip!)

2–3 cups (480–720 ml) vegetable broth, divided, plus more to thin

4 tsp (20 ml) lime juice

¾ tsp salt, or to taste

½–¾ tsp chili flakes (reduce for less heat)

¼ cup (4 g) cilantro, chopped

Preheat the oven to 425°F (218°C). Line two baking sheets with parchment paper. Arrange the carrots, onion, apple and sweet potato pieces in a single layer across the baking sheets. Drizzle with oil (if using) and season with salt and pepper. Roast until tender, about 20 to 25 minutes.

Meanwhile, put a soup pot over medium heat. Combine the curry powder, cayenne and cumin. Toast the spices in the dry pot until fragrant, stirring for about 1 minute, then add the oil, garlic and ginger. Cook and stir for another minute.

Reserve 3 tablespoons (45 ml) of coconut milk to garnish the soup. Pour the rest of the can into the pot, along with the lentils and 2 cups (480 ml) of broth. Reduce the heat and simmer for about 20 to 25 minutes, stirring occasionally, until the lentils are soft. Add more broth if the soup becomes too thick.

When the vegetables are done roasting, transfer them to a blender with the remaining cup (240 ml) of broth or water, if you prefer. Blend until smooth, about 2 minutes. Add the mixture to the pot and stir well. You can also add the roasted vegetables directly to the soup and use an immersion blender. If you use this method, be careful not to overblend if you want some texture in your soup.

Add the lime juice, salt and chili flakes. Reduce the heat and simmer for 5 to 10 minutes to allow the flavors to mingle. Add more broth or a little water to thin as needed. Taste, then adjust seasoning if desired. Ladle into serving bowls and top with chopped cilantro and a swirl of coconut milk.

FRESH TIP!

Red or yellow lentils are best for this recipe. If you use green or brown, I recommend using steamed or canned lentils (drained and rinsed).

SWEET

HOW TO MAKE PLANT-BASED FROSTING

TRADITIONAL

1 cup (205 g) of coconut shortening, 1 cup (227 g) of vegan butter, 1 cup (120 g) of powdered sugar. Beat to combine until light and fluffy!

WHOLESOME

3 cups (480 g) of pre-soaked cashews, ½ cup (120 ml) of coconut cream, ¾ cup (150 g) of coconut sugar or soft dates. Process in a food processor or high-speed blender until smooth and creamy

HOW TO MAKE NO-CHURN VEGAN ICE CREAM

2 cups (320 g) pre-soaked nuts or nut butter

1 cup (120 ml) coconut cream or full-fat coconut milk

½–1 cup (120–240 ml) sweetener—maple syrup, sweetened condensed coconut milk, dates

Optional additions—diced avocado, frozen fruit, cocoa powder, vegan marshmallows

METHOD

Blend on high until smooth and creamy, then freeze for 4 to 6 hours!

THE ART OF VEGAN BAKING AND ICE CREAM MAKING

If you have a massive sweet tooth like me, prepare to be delighted! Vegan baking and ice cream making is way more fun than the traditional stuff. It's wholesome, creative and just as delicious—minus the stomachaches and guilt!

This decadent chapter includes revamped classics like Salted Chocolate Chip Cookies (page 146) and Avocado-Mint Chip Ice Cream (page 149). There's something for every level of indulgence, from naturally sweetened Carrot Cake with Cashew Cream Cheese Frosting (page 158) to decadent showstoppers like Fudge Brownie Baked Alaska with fluffy aquafaba meringue (page 154) and mouthwatering vegan Tres Leches Cake (page 150).

Once you get the hang of baking without eggs and dairy, it becomes second nature. Here's a cheat sheet to get you started!

VEGAN TREAT CHEAT SHEET

WHEN BAKING, REPLACE 1 EGG WITH

3 tablespoons (45 ml) of aquafaba (the liquid from canned chickpeas)—delivers the lightest, fluffiest texture; it's great for cakes, cupcakes and making meringue!

SOME OTHER OPTIONS INCLUDE

1 tablespoon (7 g) of flaxseed + 2½ tablespoons (37 ml) of water—best for more wholesome or hearty foods

1 tablespoon (10 g) of chia seeds + 3 tablespoons (45 ml) of water—a little texture, great for pancakes, waffles and lemon poppy seed cakes or muffins

½ banana, mashed—great for pancakes or anytime you want to bind and add sweetness

HOW TO MAKE BUTTERMILK

1 cup (240 ml) plant-based milk (I like soy, cashew and oat) + 1 teaspoon of white or apple cider vinegar

Mix well and let thicken for 5 minutes.

SALTED CHOCOLATE CHIP COOKIES

This classic chocolate chip cookie is all grown up thanks to the addition of olive oil and flaked sea salt. Using a touch of olive oil in addition to vegan butter creates a richer flavor profile while the crunchy salt enhances the sweet, savory vibes. I love using aquafaba (the liquid in canned chickpeas) here as an egg substitute. It binds the ingredients without changing the texture in a discernible way, unlike "eggs" made from ground flaxseed, which create a denser quality in baked goods. Don't forget the plant milk for dipping!

PREP TIME: 15 MINUTES • COOK TIME: 10 MINUTES • YIELD: 24 TO 30 COOKIES

2¼ cups (281 g) all-purpose flour or gluten-free flour blend

1 tsp baking soda

1¼ tsp (7 g) sea salt

¾ cup (170 g) vegan butter, room temperature (see Fresh Tips!)

¼ cup (60 ml) extra virgin olive oil

¼ cup (50 g) granulated sugar

1 cup (220 g) brown sugar, packed

2 tsp (10 ml) vanilla extract

6 tbsp (90 ml) aquafaba

1½ cups (225 g) dark chocolate chunks

1½ cups (165 g) chopped pecans

2–3 tbsp (36–54 g) flaked sea salt (for topping)

Preheat the oven to 375°F (191°C). In a small bowl, combine the flour, baking soda and salt. In a large mixing bowl, beat the butter, oil, granulated sugar, brown sugar and vanilla extract until creamy. Add 3 tablespoons (45 ml) of the aquafaba, beat to combine, then add the remaining 3 tablespoons (45 ml) and keep mixing. Slowly add the flour mixture and beat to combine.

Roughly chop two-thirds of the chocolate chunks. Leave the rest whole. Stir the chocolate and pecans into the batter. Drop by rounded tablespoons (30 g) onto two ungreased baking sheets, 2 to 3 inches (5 to 8 cm) apart. Position the cookies so the whole chocolate chunks aren't on the bottom, or they'll stick to the pan. Press the cookie dough balls down slightly.

Bake the cookies for 9 to 12 minutes or until golden brown on the bottom. The cookies might not look fully cooked, but they'll firm up as they cool. Sprinkle each cookie with a pinch of flaked sea salt. Press the salt very gently into the cookies. Let them cool on the pan for 2 to 3 minutes, then transfer to wire racks to cool.

FRESH TIPS!

This recipe works best with margarine-style vegan butters, such as Earth Balance. If using a coconut oil–based vegan butter like Miyoko's, add a flax "egg" to the mixture to stabilize the dough. To make the flax "egg," combine 1 tablespoon (7 g) of ground flaxseed and 2½ tablespoons (37 ml) of water, then allow to thicken for 5 minutes.

Leftover dough keeps in the fridge for up to 5 days or in the freezer for up to 1 month. If working with cold cookie dough, use a melon scooper to portion the balls.

AVOCADO-MINT CHIP ICE CREAM

Mind-blowing ice cream–making tip: Blend creamy things like avocado or pre-soaked cashews with full-fat coconut milk and a can of sweetened condensed coconut milk (found in the baking section of most health food stores) to create simple, delicious, vegan ice cream. Frozen spinach adds a touch of iciness for a spot-on ice cream texture while making the ice cream a beautiful deep shade of green. Did I mention it's no-churn?

PREP TIME: 10 MINUTES • FREEZE TIME: 6 HOURS • YIELD: 8 SERVINGS

4 large ripe avocados, diced

1 cup (160 g) raw cashews, soaked for 6+ hours or boiled for 10 minutes

½ cup (120 ml) full-fat coconut milk

1 cup (240 ml) sweetened condensed coconut milk

½ cup (75 g) frozen spinach

2 tsp (10 ml) peppermint extract

1 tbsp (15 ml) lime juice

2 cups (350 g) dark chocolate chips

FOR SERVING (OPTIONAL)
Whipped Coconut Cream (page 157)

Chocolate shavings

Combine the avocados, cashews, coconut milk, condensed milk, spinach, peppermint extract and lime juice in a high-speed blender. Blend on high until completely smooth.

Add the chocolate chips. Blend on low until just incorporated, then transfer to a loaf pan. Cover tightly with cling wrap, pressing the film into the surface of the ice cream to prevent the avocado from oxidizing and changing color.

Freeze for 5 to 6 hours, then scoop and serve! The ice cream will become very firm after 12 hours in the freezer. If it's not scoopable, let it thaw on the counter to soften, about 30 minutes. Serve with whipped coconut cream and shaved chocolate (if using)!

FRESH TIPS!

For more of a Thin Mint cookie vibe, add ¼ cup (22 g) of cocoa or cacao powder when blending the ice cream, and blend a few crushed vegan chocolate sandwich cookies in with the chocolate chips! You can also add 1 tablespoon (6 g) of matcha powder for a deliciously fancy variation.

TRES LECHES CAKE

Tres Leches is a traditional Mexican sponge cake that's soaked in an insanely delicious spiced milk blend. There are a few key tricks to making fluffy sponge cake without egg whites. Trick #1—Add starch to the flour to make it lighter. Trick #2—Whip the aquafaba until it's very foamy, then gently fold into the batter. Trick #3—Grease the bottom of the pan but not the sides, so the batter can cling to the walls of the pan as it rises.

PREP TIME: 45 MINUTES • COOK TIME: 30 MINUTES, PLUS 4+ HOURS TO SOAK
YIELD: 12 SERVINGS

CAKE

1¾ cups (420 ml) non-dairy milk

2 tsp (10 ml) white vinegar

2 tsp (10 ml) vanilla extract

⅔ cup (160 ml) aquafaba
(from 1–2 cans chickpeas)

2 cups (250 g) all-purpose flour or
gluten-free flour blend

¼ cup (40 g) tapioca flour

1½ cups (300 g) cane sugar

2 tsp (10 g) baking powder

1 tsp salt

½ tsp baking soda

⅔ cup (160 ml) melted coconut oil

3 tbsp (45 ml) melted vegan butter

SPICED MILK BLEND

1 cup (240 ml) sweetened condensed
coconut milk

1 cup (240 ml) evaporated coconut
milk

¼ cup (60 ml) non-dairy milk

1 tsp cinnamon

1 tsp vanilla extract

¼ tsp ground cloves

TOPPING

2 (14-oz [400-g]) cans coconut
cream, chilled

3 tbsp (45 ml) maple syrup

½ tsp cinnamon

16 oz (453 g) strawberries, sliced

Preheat the oven to 350°F (177°C). Lightly grease the bottom of a 9 x 13–inch (23 x 33–cm) glass baking dish, avoiding the sides. In a bowl, combine the non-dairy milk, vinegar and vanilla extract. Set aside to thicken. With a mixer and balloon whisk attachment, beat the aquafaba until you achieve soft peaks, about 6 to 7 minutes.

In a large bowl, combine the flours, sugar, baking powder, salt and baking soda. Whisk thoroughly until all lumps are gone. Add the oil and vegan butter to the flour. Change the mixer attachment from the balloon to the paddle attachment. On high speed, beat the melted fats with the flour mixture until you have an even grainy texture. Slowly add the buttermilk mixture and beat until combined.

You will have a very thin and pourable cake batter. Gently fold the whipped aquafaba into the batter. Mix lightly until evenly combined but do not overmix or it will not rise properly.

Pour the batter into the baking dish. Firmly tap the pan on the counter several times to release air bubbles. Bake for 25 to 30 minutes, until the cake lightly springs back in the center when touched.

While the cake bakes, make the spiced milk blend. In a small saucepan, over medium heat, combine the condensed coconut milk, evaporated coconut milk, non-dairy milk, cinnamon, vanilla extract and cloves. Stir and bring to a light boil, then remove from the heat.

When the cake is finished baking, place it on a wire rack to cool for 10 minutes. Using a thin chopstick or 2 to 3 toothpicks, poke holes in the cake, at least every ½ inch (12 mm) or so. Pour the spiced milk blend over the cake. Cover and chill for at least 4 hours but ideally overnight to allow the cake to soak up the milk.

When the milk has mostly soaked into the cake, make the topping. Whip the chilled coconut cream with the maple syrup until smooth and fluffy. Spread the coconut cream over the cake, dust with cinnamon, then cover with strawberries. Chill for another 10 to 15 minutes to set the whipped cream, then slice and serve!

CHOCOLATE CAKE WITH AVOCADO FROSTING

Why vegan cake is better than regular cake: It's made with more wholesome ingredients, which means you can eat more of it! I swapped some of the oil for applesauce to lighten the cake and made the frosting from avocados! If avocado frosting sounds too healthy, see Fresh Tips! for a more traditional vegan chocolate buttercream.

PREP TIME: 25 MINUTES • COOK TIME: 35 MINUTES • YIELD: 12 TO 14 SERVINGS

Cooking spray

2 tsp (10 ml) white vinegar

1½ cups (360 ml) soy milk

2½ cups (313 g) all-purpose flour or gluten-free flour blend (see Fresh Tips!)

1¼ cups (110 g) cocoa powder

½ cup (60 g) potato starch (see Fresh Tips!)

1 tbsp (14 g) baking powder

2½ tsp (7 g) baking soda

1½ tsp (9 g) sea salt

2½ cups (500 g) cane or coconut sugar

1½ cups (360 ml) strong coffee

½ cup (120 ml) grapeseed or mild oil

½ cup (120 ml) aquafaba

¼ cup (64 g) applesauce

1 tbsp (15 ml) vanilla extract

FROSTING

3 cups (450 g) ripe avocado, diced

1 cup (160 g) raw cashews, soaked for 6+ hours or overnight

¾ cup (180 ml) maple syrup

⅔ cup (59 g) cocoa powder

2 tsp (10 ml) lime juice

¼ tsp sea salt

1 cup (175 g) dark chocolate chips, melted

4 cups (500 g) raspberries

Preheat the oven to 350°F (177°C). Line three 8-inch (20-cm) cake pans with parchment paper and spray with cooking oil.

In a bowl, combine the vinegar and the milk. Stir and set aside to thicken. In a large mixing bowl or stand mixer bowl, thoroughly whisk together the flour, cocoa, starch, baking powder, baking soda and sea salt. In a medium bowl, combine the sugar, coffee, oil, aquafaba, applesauce and vanilla.

Gradually add the milk mixture and coffee mixture to the dry ingredients. Beat on medium-low speed until well combined. Stop halfway and use a spatula to scrape the bottom of the bowl to make sure all the dry ingredients are incorporated. Divide the batter evenly among the cake pans. Bake for 30 to 35 minutes, until a toothpick inserted into the center comes out clean. Check at 30 minutes.

Make the frosting. Process the avocado, cashews, maple syrup, cocoa, lime juice and sea salt in a large food processor until smooth. Stop to scrape the sides as needed. Pour in the melted chocolate and process until smooth. Transfer the frosting to a bowl, cover with cling film and chill until ready to use. When the cakes are done, let them cool for 10 minutes, then invert them onto wire racks to cool completely. Pop the cakes into the freezer to cool if you're in a hurry.

Spread a third of the frosting over each cake. Place two-thirds of the raspberries evenly over two of the cakes. Arrange the rest of the raspberries evenly over the top layer. Stack the layers to build the cake. Slice and serve.

FRESH TIPS!

All-purpose flour and potato starch will deliver the lightest, fluffiest texture. For a more nutritious cake, use a gluten-free baking blend or white whole wheat flour. If using whole wheat flour, add an extra ¼ cup (60 ml) of coffee. If you don't have potato starch, substitute additional flour (not cornstarch).

VEGAN CHOCOLATE BUTTERCREAM—Beat 3 cups (615 g) of coconut shortening, 1 cup (227 g) of softened vegan butter, 1½ cups (180 g) of powdered sugar and ¼ cup (22 g) of cocoa powder until thoroughly combined.

FUDGE BROWNIE BAKED ALASKA

Behold! This epic creation is the pinnacle of plant-based dessert mastery, transforming aquafaba—
the liquid from canned chickpeas—into fluffy meringue that no one would guess is vegan! It tastes best with
bold-flavored ice cream to complement the mild, marshmallowy meringue.

PREP TIME: 30 MINUTES + 5 HOURS CHILL TIME • COOK TIME: 25 MINUTES
YIELD: 12 SERVINGS

Cooking spray

6 cups (1.4 L) vegan ice cream, slightly softened (store-bought or homemade, see Fresh Tip!)

1 cup (125 g) all-purpose flour or gluten-free flour blend

½ cup (44 g) cocoa powder

1 tsp baking powder

Scant ½ tsp salt

⅓ cup (66 g) cane or coconut sugar

¼ cup (50 g) brown sugar

½ cup (120 ml) aquafaba

½ cup (120 ml) melted coconut oil

2 tbsp (30 ml) strong coffee

2 tbsp (30 ml) non-dairy milk

1 tbsp (15 ml) vanilla extract

⅓ cup (58 g) dark chocolate chips

MERINGUE

½ cup (120 ml) aquafaba

½ tsp cream of tartar

⅓ cup (66 g) organic sugar

½ tsp xanthan gum

FRESH TIP!

If using homemade ice cream, pour the mixture directly from the blender into the lined bowl and freeze. Use a hair dryer to heat the bowl to remove the ice cream once frozen.

Spray an 8-inch (20-cm) shallow mixing bowl with cooking oil. Line with cling wrap. Scoop the ice cream into the bowl. Press it down and smooth out the top. Freeze for 4 hours or overnight.

Preheat the oven to 350°F (177°C). Lightly oil a round 8-inch (20-cm) cake pan. Line the bottom with parchment paper.

In a large bowl, whisk together the flour, cocoa, baking powder and salt. In a smaller bowl, beat together the cane sugar, brown sugar, aquafaba, coconut oil, coffee, milk and vanilla extract. Combine the wet and dry ingredients. Mix until smooth, then add the chocolate chips.

Pour the batter into the pan. Bake for 20 to 25 minutes, until a toothpick inserted into the center comes out clean. Cool on a wire rack for 10 to 15 minutes, then carefully remove the brownie from the pan and place it in the freezer to cool it completely, about 15 to 20 minutes. Once fully cooled, place the brownie on top of the ice cream. Cover and freeze for 30 minutes.

Meanwhile, make the meringue. Pour the aquafaba and cream of tartar into the bowl of a stand mixer fitted with the balloon whisk attachment. Mix on medium-high until frothy, about 3 to 4 minutes. Process the sugar in a mini processor for 1 minute, until it's fine like caster sugar.

When the aquafaba is frothy, add the sugar 1 tablespoon (12 g) at a time. Keep mixing for 5 to 7 minutes, until stiff peaks form. Add the xanthan gum. This helps the meringue remain stiff. Mix for another minute, then place your serving plate over the brownie and flip it upside down to release the ice cream.

Spoon the meringue over the dessert in a thick, even layer, forming pretty peaks. Freeze for another 30 minutes, uncovered. Torch with a kitchen torch until the peaks are browned. Serve right away.

If you don't have a torch, broil the dessert for 30 seconds on a rack in the upper third of the oven. This method browns the top more than the sides, but it's a decent alternative. Be sure to cover the entire cake in meringue, forming a seal along the bottom edge of the cake to keep the ice cream from getting melty in the oven.

LEMON POPPY SEED PANCAKES

Chia "eggs" are my favorite egg replacer for pancakes. They make the pancakes nice and fluffy while adding a hint of crunch that's so damn satisfying. Lemon poppy seed pancakes are my fave, but check out Fresh Tips! for variations like blueberry, chocolate chip and banana walnut. For a decadent, impressive brunch, top the pancakes with plenty of whipped coconut cream (store-bought or see Fresh Tips! for recipe).

PREP TIME: 15 MINUTES • COOK TIME: 10 MINUTES • YIELD: 4 SERVINGS

1 tbsp (10 g) chia seeds

3 tbsp (45 ml) water

1 tsp + ¼ cup (65 ml) lemon juice, divided

1½ cups (360 ml) soy milk

2 cups (250 g) white whole wheat flour or gluten-free flour blend

¼ cup (50 g) coconut sugar

4 tsp (18 g) baking powder

¼ tsp baking soda

½ tsp salt

¼ cup (60 ml) melted vegan butter, plus more to grease the pan

1 tsp vanilla extract

Zest of 2 lemons, divided

1 tbsp (9 g) poppy seeds

FOR SERVING

1 cup (240 ml) whipped coconut cream (store-bought or see Fresh Tips!)

1 cup (120 g) fresh raspberries

1 cup (240 ml) maple syrup

In a small bowl, combine the chia seeds and water. Set aside. This will be your egg replacer. In another bowl, combine 1 teaspoon of lemon juice and the milk. Set aside. The acidity curdles the milk slightly to form vegan "buttermilk." Reserve the rest of the lemon juice for the pancakes.

In a large bowl, whisk together the flour, sugar, baking powder, baking soda and salt. Make a well in the center. In the center, add the "buttermilk," chia "egg," melted butter, remaining ¼ cup (60 ml) of lemon juice and vanilla. Whisk together the wet ingredients within the well before gently folding in the dry ingredients. Mix until mostly smooth. Some lumps are okay. Reserve ½ teaspoon lemon zest for garnish, and stir the rest into the batter along with the poppy seeds.

Preheat a griddle pan over medium-high heat for 2 minutes, then reduce the heat to medium-low. Grease the pan with vegan butter.

Scoop ¼ cup (60 ml) of batter onto the hot griddle at a time. When the bottoms are golden brown and there are several air bubbles in the pancakes, flip them over. Cook for 2 to 3 minutes on each side, until golden brown and crisp.

Serve with whipped coconut cream, raspberries, reserved lemon zest and maple syrup.

FRESH TIPS!

For different variations, omit the lemon zest, poppy seeds and ¼ cup (60 ml) of the lemon juice. You'll still need 1 teaspoon of lemon juice for the buttermilk. Increase the soy milk to 1¾ cups (420 ml). Add blueberries, chocolate chips or sliced bananas and chopped walnuts to the batter.

WHIPPED COCONUT CREAM——Chill 1 (14-oz [400-g]) can of coconut cream for several hours or overnight. Once chilled, open and drain the excess liquid. You can save it for a smoothie! In a bowl, combine the chilled cream with 3 tablespoons (45 ml) of maple syrup or 3 tablespoons (24 g) of powdered sugar. Whip with a hand mixer until fluffy, about 3 to 5 minutes. Store in a closed container in the fridge for up to 5 days.

CARROT CAKE WITH CASHEW CREAM CHEESE FROSTING

I love this guilt-free cake! It's whole wheat, naturally sweetened, and the frosting is made from nuts. Whole wheat pastry flour is finely ground, which keeps the cake nice and light. Applesauce replaces some of the oil while keeping the cake moist. The unique method of layering the cake is foolproof for all baking novices and delivers seriously impressive results, but you can always make a simple sheet cake if preferred.

PREP TIME: 30 MINUTES • COOK TIME: 22 MINUTES • YIELD: 12 SERVINGS

2 cups (240 g) whole wheat pastry flour or gluten-free flour blend

1½ tbsp (12 g) cinnamon

2 tsp (9 g) baking powder

2 tsp (3 g) ground ginger

1 tsp baking soda

1 tsp salt

1 tsp nutmeg

1 tsp allspice

1½ cups (300 g) coconut sugar

½ cup (120 ml) aquafaba

¾ cup (180 ml) melted coconut oil

½ cup (125 g) applesauce

¼ cup (60 ml) non-dairy milk

2 tbsp (40 g) molasses

1 tsp vanilla extract

3 cups (330 g) grated carrots

1 cup (125 g) chopped walnuts

CASHEW CREAM CHEESE FROSTING

3 cups (480 g) raw cashews, soaked for 6+ hours or boiled for 10 minutes

½ cup (120 ml) melted coconut oil

⅓ cup (80 ml) maple syrup

1 tsp apple cider vinegar

¼ tsp lemon zest

Pinch of salt

FOR GARNISH

½ cup (65 g) pecans

OPTIONAL EQUIPMENT FOR NAKED LAYER CAKE

6-inch (15-cm) springform pan

2 sheets clear acetate

Preheat the oven to 350°F (177°C). Oil a 9 x 13–inch (23 x 33–cm) pan. Line the bottom with parchment paper.

In a large bowl, whisk together the flour, cinnamon, baking powder, ginger, baking soda, salt, nutmeg and allspice. In a second bowl, combine the sugar, aquafaba, coconut oil, applesauce, milk, molasses and vanilla. Fold the wet ingredients into the dry ingredients until just incorporated. Mix in the carrots and walnuts. The batter will be very thick.

Spread the batter evenly in the pan. Bake for 22 to 25 minutes, until a toothpick inserted into the center comes out clean. Check at 22 minutes.

Make the frosting. In a high-speed blender, blend the cashews, coconut oil, syrup, vinegar, lemon zest and salt. This makes a very creamy frosting but requires a bit of effort. Use the tamper and stop frequently to scrape down the sides.

Line a cutting board with parchment paper. When the cake is done, cool completely, then transfer to the cutting board. Use the ring of the springform pan to cut out two circles and two half circles from the cake. Clasp the bottom of the pan into the ring. Line with parchment paper. Place the acetate sheets on the inside of the ring to form the cake mold.

Place the half circles and cake scraps into the pan to form the bottom layer. Cover with one-third of the frosting. Layer another cake circle on top, followed by one-third of the frosting, then repeat. Decorate the top with pecans. Cover well and freeze overnight to set. Remove the acetate when frozen and allow to the cake to thaw on the counter for 2 to 3 hours before serving.

WORLD-FAMOUS MACADAMIA NUT ICE CREAM

This decadent treat is a plant-based version of the Macadamia Nut Ice Cream at the world-famous Bern's Steak House in my hometown, Tampa, Florida. Legend has it that the founder spent seven years perfecting the recipe, making over 300 versions to get it just right. I've been craving this ice cream ever since going vegan, so I finally re-created it for this book. After several attempts myself, I got to taste the ice cream I so fondly remembered. Infusing the roasted nuts with milk and sugar on the stove creates a deep nutty flavor, which is enhanced by just a hint of cocoa. I love serving it as ice cream, but it also works as a no-bake cheesecake, or for major bonus points, make it into ice cream sandwiches using the Salted Chocolate Chip Cookies (page 146). See Fresh Tips! for no-bake cheesecake and sandwich methods!

> **PREP TIME: 20 MINUTES • FREEZE TIME: 6+ HOURS • YIELD: 4 TO 6 SERVINGS**

2½ cups (335 g) roasted unsalted macadamia nuts

1½ cups (360 ml) soy milk

2 tbsp (25 g) brown sugar

2 tsp (10 ml) vanilla extract

1 cup (240 ml) sweetened condensed coconut milk

1½ cups (360 ml) coconut cream, plus more to thin if needed

2 tsp (3 g) cocoa powder

FOR SERVING (OPTIONAL)

1 cup (240 ml) Whipped Coconut Cream (page 157)

½ cup (60 g) chocolate shavings

Roughly chop the nuts. To save time, you can pulse them several times in a food processor until chopped. Reserve ½ cup (67 g) of nuts. Put the rest in a saucepan, along with the milk and brown sugar. Bring to a strong simmer, between medium and medium-low heat, and simmer until the milk is absorbed, about 10 minutes.

Place the infused nuts, vanilla, condensed coconut milk, coconut cream and cocoa powder in a high-speed blender. Blend on high for several minutes, until the ice cream is smooth and creamy. You will need to use the tamper continuously and stop to scrape down the sides. If the mixture is too thick to blend, add a bit more coconut cream, 1 to 2 tablespoons (15 to 30 ml) at a time.

Pour the mixture into a freezer-safe container. I like to use a mini loaf pan. Stir in the remaining roasted nuts, saving a few to garnish the top. Press the ice cream down into the pan. Use the back of a spoon to create swirls in the top, then sprinkle with the reserved nuts. Cover and freeze for 6 hours, or ideally overnight, then serve. The ice cream is fabulous served on its own but even better with whipped coconut cream and chocolate shavings (if using).

FRESH TIPS!

Swap in hazelnuts or chopped brazil nuts for macadamia nuts as desired.

Another fun way to eat this treat is to serve it as no-bake cheesecake. Pour the ice cream into a chocolate pie crust, then freeze and serve. You can also pour the ice cream into a wide, lined pan, then cut out circles with a biscuit cutter that is similar in size to your Salted Chocolate Chip Cookies (page 146). Place the circles of ice cream between two cookies to make easy vegan ice cream sandwiches.

This recipes tastes absolutely incredible when paired with Carrot Cake (page 158). Serve the cake à la mode or use the blended macadamia cream in place of the cashew cream cheese frosting.

GOOEY CHOCOLATE BANANA CAKE

Look Ma, no eggs! Banana acts as a binder in this irresistible, kinda-sorta healthy dessert. It bakes super moist, especially in the center. The end result is very chocolatey, decadent and ooey-gooey—just how I like it!

PREP TIME: 15 MINUTES • COOK TIME: 50 MINUTES • YIELD: 8 TO 10 SERVINGS

⅔ cup + 2 tbsp (160 g) coconut or brown sugar, divided

⅓ cup (75 g) vegan butter, softened

2 tsp (10 ml) vanilla extract

4 medium-size very ripe bananas

1½ cups (188 g) white whole wheat or all-purpose flour

1 tsp cinnamon

1 tsp baking soda

½ tsp salt

½–¾ cup (88–131 g) dark chocolate chips or any dairy-free version, divided (see Fresh Tips!)

½ cup (63 g) chopped walnuts (optional)

Preheat the oven to 350°F (177°C). Grease a metal loaf pan with butter.

In a medium bowl, cream together the ⅔ cup (135 g) of sugar, butter and vanilla. Slice 1 banana in half vertically. Set aside 1 piece to top the banana cake, then mash the remaining 3½ bananas. Add the mashed banana to the sugar mixture. Mix well.

In a separate bowl, whisk together the flour, cinnamon, baking soda and salt. Fold the dry ingredients into the banana mixture. Stir until well combined. Reserve 2 tablespoons (20 g) of chocolate chips and mix the rest into the batter, along with the nuts (if using).

Pour the batter into the loaf pan. Smooth out the top, place the vertical slice of banana in the center, cut side up, then sprinkle with the remaining sugar and chocolate chips. Bake for 45 to 50 minutes, until a toothpick inserted into the center comes out clean. Cool on a wire rack. While warm, the center may appear under-baked. Slice and serve once cooled. You can speed this up by popping it in the fridge or freezer for a few minutes.

FRESH TIPS!

If using a silicone baking pan, you may need to increase the bake time by a few minutes.

To reduce sweetness, use ½ cup (88 g) of chocolate chips. For a richer cake, use the full ¾ cup (131 g).

OPTIONAL SWAPS—You can use gluten-free all-purpose flour if needed. Use mini chips instead of regular if preferred. You can also swap in coconut oil for the vegan butter.

CLASSIC APPLE PIE

Tips for making a truly incredible classic apple pie: #1—Make the crust with vodka! It evaporates when cooking, making the crust extra flaky. #2—Cook the pie on the bottom shelf. This will prevent a soggy crust. #3—Precook the apples. This makes for a gooier pie with softer apples, similar to the kind you'd find in a bakery or store. I like to use a blend of tart and sweet apples, or whichever are local and in season!

PREP TIME: 45 MINUTES • COOK TIME: 55 MINUTES • YIELD: 8 SERVINGS

CRUST

2½ cups (313 g) all-purpose, whole wheat pastry or gluten-free flour, plus more for rolling

1 tsp salt

1 tbsp (12 g) coconut sugar

¾ cup (170 g) vegan butter, cut into small pieces, plus more to grease the pan

¼ cup (60 ml) ice-cold water

¼ cup (60 ml) ice-cold vodka

APPLE FILLING

4 lbs (1.8 kg) apples

4 tsp (20 ml) lemon juice

3 tbsp (24 g) whole wheat pastry flour or gluten-free flour blend

½ cup (100 g) coconut sugar

⅓ cup (70 g) brown sugar

1¼ tsp (3 g) cinnamon

¼ tsp nutmeg

¼ tsp allspice

2 tbsp (28 g) vegan butter

2 tbsp (30 ml) apple cider

1 tbsp (15 ml) aquafaba

2 tsp (8 g) coarse sugar (optional)

FOR SERVING

4 cups (600 g) vegan vanilla ice cream

½ tsp cinnamon

Preheat the oven to 425°F (218°C) with a rack in the lower third of the oven.

Make the crust. Place the flour, salt, sugar and vegan butter in a food processor. Process until a grainy, even crumb forms. Pour the water and vodka in while the machine is running. It will form a large ball in the processor. Scrape down the sides if needed.

Shape the dough into a large ball. Divide it into two balls, one slightly larger than the other. Cover with cling film and chill for 30 minutes.

Meanwhile, make the apple filling. Peel and slice the apples into ¼-inch (6-mm)-thick half moons. In a bowl, toss them with lemon juice. In another bowl, combine the flour, coconut sugar, brown sugar, cinnamon, nutmeg and allspice. Toss the apples in the spice mixture and set aside for 5 minutes.

In a very large frying pan, over medium heat, melt the butter. Add the apples, mixing thoroughly to incorporate the butter. Cook for 1 to 2 minutes until the apples begin to soften slightly, then add the cider. Stir well. Cook until the apples are softened and a gooey cinnamon coating forms, 5 to 7 minutes, stirring occasionally.

While the apples finish up, grease the pie pan with butter and flour. Roll out the larger ball of dough to 12 inches (30 cm) in diameter, then carefully line the bottom of the pan with the dough. Let the edges hang over, then trim the excess. Put the apples in the pie crust. Smooth the top into a rounded, even layer. Roll out the remaining dough to 9 inches (23 cm) in diameter. Place it on top of the apples. Fold the bottom edges over and crimp the edges of the dough together with a fork. Use your fingers to shape the crust. With a sharp paring knife, cut 3 to 4 slits in the top of the pie so the steam can escape. You can also cut fun shapes or get creative with it.

Brush the top of the dough with the aquafaba and sprinkle with the coarse sugar (if using). Bake at 425°F (218°C) for 15 minutes, then reduce the oven temperature to 350°F (177°C) and bake for another 40 minutes. Tent the edges of the pie with foil when there are 15 minutes left so the edges don't burn.

When it's done, let the pie sit for 20 minutes, or ideally overnight. Slice and serve warm with plant-based vanilla ice cream and a sprinkle of cinnamon.

ORANGE BLOSSOM CHIA PUDDING

Orange blossom syrup is the key to this unbelievably light, flavorful, downright DREAMY chia pudding. The floral notes of the orange blossom combined with the creamy coconut milk give this simple chia pudding a luxurious flavor and mouthfeel. Find orange blossom syrup at Indian markets or online. One bottle will last for several months!

PREP TIME: 5 MINUTES • CHILL TIME: 55 MINUTES • YIELD: 4 SERVINGS

1 cup (240 ml) full-fat coconut milk

1 cup (240 ml) soy milk

¼ cup (60 ml) agave nectar

1 tbsp (15 ml) orange blossom syrup

½ cup (81 g) chia seeds

FOR SERVING

2 ripe mangos, diced

1 cup (123 g) berries of choice

A few sprigs of mint (optional, for garnish)

In a container with a lid, whisk together the coconut milk, soy milk, agave nectar and orange blossom syrup. Add the chia seeds, close the lid and shake well. Place in the fridge for 5 to 10 minutes, then uncover and stir well.

Let the pudding thicken in the fridge for another 30 to 45 minutes, or for a few hours or overnight for a thicker pudding. Serve with mango, berries and a sprig of mint.

FRESH TIPS!

For a thicker pudding, chill the chia pudding overnight.

PEANUT BUTTER AND JELLY ICE CREAM

You're going to love this classic childhood treat reimagined as no-churn vegan ice cream! The chunky date pieces add a natural sweetness and scrumptious chewiness, while the combination of peanut butter and frozen strawberries gives the ice cream a creamy, frosty texture. And who doesn't love a thick jelly swirl? Freeze the ice cream in a shallow pan and cut circles out with a biscuit cutter. Layer the circles between two cookies to make easy ice cream sandwiches!

PREP TIME: 15 MINUTES • FREEZE TIME: 4 TO 6 HOURS • YIELD: 6 SERVINGS

¼ cup (5 g) freeze-dried strawberries

¾ cup (190 g) peanut butter (with salt), divided

16 oz (453 g) frozen strawberries

1 cup (225 g) soft Medjool dates (see Fresh Tips!)

½ cup (120 ml) full-fat coconut milk, plus more if needed

2 tbsp (30 ml) maple syrup or agave nectar (optional, for added sweetness)

1 tbsp (15 ml) water

2 tsp (10 ml) lemon juice

¼ cup (80 g) strawberry jelly

FOR SERVING (OPTIONAL)
Whipped Coconut Cream (page 157)
Roasted peanuts, chopped

Rehydrate the freeze-dried strawberries with a little warm water and set aside.

Reserve 2 tablespoons (32 g) of peanut butter. Then place the rest of the peanut butter in a high-speed blender, along with the frozen strawberries, dates and coconut milk. Blend on high until creamy and fluffy, with tiny but visible date morsels remaining, about 4 to 5 minutes. Push the ice cream down with the tamper continuously while blending, or stop to scrape down the sides if using a processor. Give the machine breaks if needed. Taste, then add the maple syrup if you'd like it to be a little sweeter.

For smoother ice cream, keep blending until the dates are fully incorporated. Add more coconut milk 1 tablespoon (15 ml) at a time if needed to blend, but keep in mind that this will thin the finished product.

Squeeze the water from the freeze-dried strawberries, then chop them into fine pieces. Add them to the blender and blend on low until just incorporated into the ice cream.

Mix the water and lemon juice into the jelly to make it swirlable and a little tangy. Transfer the ice cream to a small baking dish. Swirl the jelly and remaining 2 tablespoons (32 g) of peanut butter into the ice cream. Serve right away as soft serve or freeze for 4 to 6 hours for scoopable ice cream. Serve with whipped coconut cream and chopped roasted peanuts (if using)!

FRESH TIPS!

If your dates aren't super soft and sticky, soak them in hot water for 15 minutes before using, then drain.

This ice cream tastes best if consumed within 1 to 2 days. After 24 hours in the freezer, this ice cream becomes EXTREMELY solid. Allow it to thaw on the counter for 30 to 45 minutes before serving if it's too firm to scoop.

NO-BAKE PURPLE SWEET POTATO PIE

Reasons to love this dessert: It's no-bake, so very low fuss. It's made from sweet potato—a vegetable—which means it's basically a salad. And it's PURPLE, which I think we can all agree just makes food taste better. Good ol' orange sweet potatoes and yams work just fine if that's convenient.

PREP TIME: 20 MINUTES • FREEZE TIME: 4+ HOURS • YIELD: 8 SERVINGS

---

1 very large sweet potato, about 5 cups (670 g) chopped (purple if you can find it!)

CRUST
2 cups (220 g) pecans

1½ cups (340 g) sticky Medjool dates (see Fresh Tip!)

1½ cups (135 g) oats

½ tsp cinnamon

Scant ½ tsp salt

3 tbsp (45 ml) maple syrup

FILLING
1½ cups (240 g) raw cashews, soaked for 6+ hours or boiled for 10 minutes

½ cup (100 g) golden coconut sugar or light brown sugar

1½ tsp (3 g) minced ginger

1 tsp cinnamon

¼ tsp nutmeg

1 cup (240 ml) full-fat coconut milk

2 tbsp (30 ml) maple syrup

FOR SERVING
2 cups (480 ml) whipped coconut cream (store-bought or page 157)

¼ tsp cinnamon

Line an 8-inch (20-cm) springform pan with parchment paper. Put a medium pot of water on to boil. Peel and chop the sweet potato into 1-inch (2.5-cm) pieces. Boil until fork-tender, about 6 to 7 minutes.

Meanwhile, make the crust. Process the pecans, dates, oats, cinnamon and salt in a large food processor until you have a coarse, even texture. Pour in the maple syrup and process until you have a thick, sticky dough. Press the dough evenly into the bottom of the springform pan to create the crust.

Make the filling. In a high-speed blender, combine the cooked sweet potato, cashews, sugar, ginger, cinnamon, nutmeg, milk and maple syrup. Blend until very smooth and creamy, about 3 to 5 minutes. Stir often with the tamper to ensure the mixture blends evenly.

Pour the sweet potato mixture into the crust. Spread into an even layer. Cover and freeze for 4 hours or overnight. Let thaw for 20 minutes before serving. Garnish with the whipped coconut cream and a sprinkle of cinnamon.

FRESH TIP!

If your dates are firm, soak them in hot water for 10 minutes to soften before using, then drain.

ACKNOWLEDGMENTS

Thank you so much to everyone who supported my first book, *30-Minute Vegan Dinners*! It was a dream come true becoming a published author, and I'm so grateful for the opportunity to do it a second time.

Thank you to Pasha and Lily for making life so magical.

Thank you to my publisher Will, my editor Sarah and the many talented folks at Page Street for helping me create this beautiful book! I so appreciate the guidance, creative freedom and support you've given me over the last few years. You're the best!

Thank you to my recipe testers for making sure each recipe can be perfectly re-created every time! I love each and every one of you. Special shout-out to everyone who tested over 15 recipes!

Maynard Madsen (bonus points for testing 47 recipes!)
Jen Hamer
Malissa de Jager
Ally Levine
Jessica Soul
Melissa Carter
Rachel Jones
Marie-Lou Roeyaerts
Megan Gunter
Laurianne Audet

Scarlet Eskew
Bev Mattheson
Brittany Cripps
Abby Ramey
Taryn Meyer
Alana Halden
Patty Mondo
Skye Davis
Liliana Lopez
Kristin Malotke

Big hugs to all of my fans and followers of Carrots & Flowers. I am where I am because you all loved my content, made my recipes and shared my videos. Thank you so, so much for your support!

I want to thank my uber-talented mom, Linda Knight, for making such incredible illustrations for this book!

And finally, I want to thank everyone in the plant-based community and beyond for inspiring me with your drive, activism and overall dedication to making the world a better place.

ABOUT THE AUTHOR

Megan Sadd is a chef, writer and lifelong lover of plant-based cuisine. In 2015, Megan combined her passion for vegan cooking with her experience in the entertainment industry to create Carrots & Flowers, an inspired vegan blog and one of the top plant-based cooking channels on Facebook. Her first book, *30-Minute Vegan Dinners*, was featured by Forbes as one of the best healthy cookbooks of the year. She has been featured on national TV, and in the *Washington Post*, *Thrive* magazine, *VegNews* magazine, *Women's Health* and HuffPost.

Megan lives in Los Angeles, where she balances blogging and #momlife with freelance TV projects, developing restaurant menus and prioritizing fun. Her favorite things include skinny palm trees, radical self-care and making vegan cheese.

Follow Megan on Instagram @carrotsandflowers and @megansadd. For more recipes, go to carrotsandflowers.com and watch her videos on her Facebook page, Carrots & Flowers.

INDEX